Common Prayer

Common Prayer

Reflections on Episcopal Worship

Edited by
Joseph S. Pagano
and Amy E. Richter

Foreword by
Stanley Hauerwas

CASCADE *Books* · Eugene, Oregon

COMMON PRAYER
Reflections on Episcopal Worship

Cascade Books
An Imprint of Wipf and Stock Publishers
199 W. 8th Ave., Suite 3
Eugene, OR 97401

www.wipfandstock.com

PAPERBACK ISBN: 978-1-5326-5422-0
HARDCOVER ISBN: 978-1-5326-5423-7
EBOOK ISBN: 978-1-5326-5424-4

Cataloguing-in-Publication data:

Names: Pagano, Joseph S., Ph.D., editor. | Richter, Amy E., editor. | Hauerwas, Stanley, 1940–, foreword writer.

Title: Common prayer : reflections on Episcopal worship / edited by Joseph S. Pagano and Amy E. Richter; foreword by Stanley Hauerwas.

Description: Eugene, OR: Cascade Books, 2019 | Includes bibliographical references.

Identifiers: ISBN 978-1-5326-5422-0 (paperback) | ISBN 978-1-5326-5423-7 (hardcover) | ISBN 978-1-5326-5424-4 (ebook)

Subjects: LCSH: Episcopal Church—Liturgy | Public worship—Episcopal Church | Worship | Anglican communion—United States

Classification: BX5940 P34 2019 (paperback) | BX5940 (ebook)

Manufactured in the U.S.A.   03/13/19

This book is dedicated to the College of Transfiguration in Makhanda/Grahamstown, South Africa

Contents

Permissions

Spencer Reece's essay originally appeared in the September 21, 2018 issue of *Commonweal*.

Lauren F. Winner's essay originally appeared in the journal *Image 96*.

A portion of Rodney Clapp's essay originally appeared in the April 6, 2010 issue of *The Christian Century*.

Fred Bahnson's essay originally appeared in longer form in the December 2016 issue of *Harper's* magazine.

Unless otherwise noted, all Scripture quotations are from New Revised Standard Version Bible, copyright © 1989 National Council of Churches of Christ in the United States of America. Used by permission. All rights reserved worldwide.

In Sophfronia Scott's essay, the Scripture quoted is from the Good News Bible © 1994 published by the Bible Societies/HarperCollins Publishers Ltd UK, Good News Bible © American Bible Society 1966, 1971, 1976, 1992. Used with permission.

Contributors

J. Neil Alexander is a bishop of The Episcopal Church and presently serves as Dean, Professor of Liturgy, and Charles Todd Quintard Professor of Theology in the School of Theology of the University of the South, Sewanee, Tennessee.

Fred Bahnson is the author of *Soil & Sacrament* and co-author with Norman Wirzba of *Making Peace with the Land*. His essays have appeared in *Harper's, Oxford American, Image, Orion, The Sun, Washington Post*, and *Best American Spiritual Writing*. He is the recipient of the Pilgrimage Essay Award, a W. K. Kellogg Food & Community fellowship, and a North Carolina Artist fellowship in creative nonfiction from the NC Arts Council. He is on the faculty at Wake Forest University School of Divinity.

Michael Battle is the Herbert Thompson Professor of Church and Society and Director of the Desmond Tutu Center at General Theological Seminary in New York. He was ordained a priest by Archbishop Desmond Tutu in 1993. Battle has published nine books, including *Reconciliation: The Ubuntu Theology of Desmond Tutu*, and the book for The Episcopal Church's General Convention, *Ubuntu: I in You and You in Me*.

Luisa E. Bonillas lives in Arizona with her family. She received her bachelor's degree from Wellesley College and her PhD from Arizona State University. Her focus was twentieth-century American

History and her dissertation topic was a History of Women of Color at Wellesley College, 1966–2001. Luisa joined The Episcopal Church in 1996 and has worked for a mission, parish, cathedral, diocese, and the wider church. She has attended numerous general conventions and has participated as a member of councils, commissions, and committees on Diocesan and church-wide levels.

Rodney Clapp is an editor at Cascade Books. He is the author of several award-winning books, including *A Peculiar People: Church as Culture in a Post-Christian Society* and *Tortured Wonders: Christian Spirituality for People, Not Angels*. His most recent book is *New Creation: A Primer on Living in the Time between the Times*. He and his wife pray at St. Barnabas Episcopal Church, Glen Ellyn, Illinois.

Melissa Deckman Fallon is the Louis L. Goldstein Professor of Public Affairs at Washington College. She also chairs the board and is an Affiliated Scholar of the Public Religion Research Institute (PRRI). Professor Deckman Fallon's areas of specialty include gender, religion, and political behavior. The author of more than a dozen scholarly articles and several books, her latest book is *Tea Party Women: Mama Grizzlies, Grassroots Leaders, and the Changing Face of the American Right*.

Kim Edwards is the author of two novels, *The Memory Keeper's Daughter* and *The Lake of Dreams*, as well as the story collection *The Secrets of a Fire King*. She and her husband have two grown daughters. Kim divides her time between Lexington, Kentucky and Seneca Falls, New York; she is finishing a new novel, *Lionfish*.

Stephen Fowl is Professor of Theology and Dean of Loyola College of Arts and Sciences at Loyola University Maryland in Baltimore, MD. Steve and his family worship at the Cathedral of the Incarnation in Baltimore. An active lay person, Steve preaches and teaches in parishes around the country. He also serves on the House of

Bishop's Theology Committee and has published numerous academic volumes on the New Testament.

Paul Fromberg is the rector of St. Gregory of Nyssa Episcopal Church in San Francisco. He teaches at the Church Divinity School of the Pacific, and for The Episcopal Church in Minnesota. Paul is also a consultant, retreat leader, and mentor. He is The Episcopal Church's representative for the Consultation on Common Texts and a member of the Standing Commission on Music and Liturgy. He is the author of *The Art of Transformation*.

Kathryn Greene-McCreight is an affiliate priest at Christ Church, New Haven and serves as a spiritual director to Saint Hilda's House. She is also an Annand mentor to students at Berkeley Divinity School at Yale Divinity School. Her most recent books include *Darkness Is My Only Companion: A Christian Response to Mental Illness* and *I Am With You: The Archbishop of Canterbury's Lent Book 2016*. She is co-chair of the Patient and Family Advisory Council of Yale-New Haven Psychiatric Hospital, and is on the board of the Elm City Affiliate of NAMI (National Alliance on Mental Illness). She has two adult children, and lives with her husband and goldendoodle in New Haven.

Cameron Dezen Hammon is a writer and musician whose work has appeared in *Ecotone, The Rumpus, The Literary Review, The Butter, Brevity's Nonfiction Blog, The Houston Chronicle*, and elsewhere. Her essay "Infirmary Music" was named notable in *The Best American Essays 2017*, and she is the host of *The Ish* podcast. Her first book, *This Is My Body: A Memoir of Religious and Romantic Obsession*, will be published by Lookout Books in 2019.

Stanley Hauerwas is Gilbert T. Rowe Professor Emeritus of Divinity at Duke University. He was named "America's Best Theologian" by *Time* magazine in 2001, the same year that he delivered the Gifford Lectureship at the University of St. Andrews, Scotland. His book, *A Community of Character: Toward a Constructive Christian*

Social Ethic, was selected as one of the 100 most important books on religion of the twentieth century.

BJ Heyboer is priest of two rural parishes in the Episcopal Diocese of Western Michigan. She has an MDiv from The School of Theology, The University of the South. Prior to ordination, BJ worked for more than twenty years in religious book publishing, most recently as cofounder of Brazos Press and senior marketing director for books published by Brazos and Baker Academic.

Rhonda Mawhood Lee is a priest, writer, and spiritual director. She currently serves as a canon to the bishop of North Carolina.

Ian S. Markham is the Dean and President of Virginia Theological Seminary and Professor of Theology and Ethics. He has degrees from the King's College London, the University of Cambridge, and the University of Exeter. He is the author of many books, including *Liturgical Life Principles* and *Understanding Christian Doctrine*. He is a priest associate at St. Paul's Episcopal Church in Old Town Alexandria, VA. He is married to Lesley and has one son, Luke.

Duane Alexander Miller is a native of Montana but has lived and ministered in many places, including Mexico, Jordan, Israel, and Spain. He is married to Sharon and they have three young children. They live in Madrid where Duane serves as a priest at the Anglican Cathedral of the Redeemer and is an associate professor at the Protestant Faculty of Theology (UEBE). Duane holds a PhD in divinity from the University of Edinburgh and has published broadly on the topics of ex-Muslim Christians and the history of Anglicanism in the Middle East.

Joseph S. Pagano currently serves as an appointed missionary of The Episcopal Church. He is visiting lecturer in theology at the College of Transfiguration in Makhanda/Grahamstown, South Africa. He is married to Amy Richter.

Amy Peterson is the author of *Dangerous Territory: My Misguided Quest to Save the World*. She's at work on a book reimagining virtues for our current political moment. Amy has taught college courses since 2003. She has an MA in intercultural studies from Wheaton and an MFA in creative writing from Seattle Pacific University. Amy and her family are members of Gethsemane Episcopal Church in Marion, Indiana.

Spencer Reece is the author of *The Clerk's Tale* and *The Road to Emmaus*. In 2017 he edited an anthology of poems by abandoned girls in a home called Our Little Roses in San Pedro Sula, Honduras: *Counting Time Like People Count Stars*. A book of prose, sixteen years in the making, *The Little Entrance: Devotions*, mixing autobiography with literary appreciation of poets, will be out by 2020. In 2012 he founded the Unamuno Author Series in Madrid, Spain.

Amy E. Richter currently serves as an appointed missionary of The Episcopal Church. She is the author of *Enoch and the Gospel of Matthew* and is visiting lecturer in biblical studies at the College of Transfiguration in Makhanda/Grahamstown, South Africa. She is married to Joseph Pagano.

C. K. Robertson is Canon to the Presiding Bishop for Ministry Beyond The Episcopal Church and Distinguished Visiting Professor at General Theological Seminary. A life member of the Council on Foreign Relations as well as other national and international boards, Dr. Robertson interacts extensively with the U.S. Department of State and Members of Congress, and previously worked with the White House and U.S. Department of Education as Executive Director of *Film Clips for Character Education*. He serves as General Editor of the Studies in Episcopal and Anglican Theology series through Peter Lang Publishing, and has written over a dozen books, including *Barnabas vs. Paul* and *A Dangerous Dozen*.

Sophfronia Scott is author of an essay collection (*Love's Long Line*), a memoir (*This Child of Faith: Raising a Spiritual Child in a Secular World*), and two novels (*Unforgivable Love* and *All I Need to Get By*). Sophfronia teaches at Regis University's Mile-High MFA and Bay Path University's MFA in Creative Nonfiction. Her family attends Trinity Episcopal Church in Newtown, Connecticut. She blogs at www.Sophfronia.com.

Rachel Marie Stone teaches English and helps run a girls' dorm at a boarding school on Long Island, NY. She is the author of four books, including the award-winning *Eat With Joy: Redeeming God's Gift of Food*, and, most recently, *Birthing Hope*, a memoir on motherhood and anxiety.

Lauren F. Winner is the vicar of Saint Paul's Episcopal Church in Louisburg, North Carolina, and a professor at Duke Divinity School. Her books include *Girl Meets God, Mudhouse Sabbath, A Cheerful and Comfortable Faith, Still: Notes on a Mid-Faith Crisis, Wearing God*, and most recently *The Dangers of Christian Practice*.

Foreword

Stanley Hauerwas

We believe as Christians what we do in liturgy is not some attempt to convince ourselves that worship avoids being just another exercise in groupthink. Rather we believe what we do liturgically is a truthful practice. If we did not know how to worship God we would have no way to know what it means to say and live the truth that is Christ. So liturgy is not just something else Christians do. Liturgy makes us Christians.

If what we do liturgically is not true then we are people who are literally lost in the cosmos. But the good news is that the cosmos is storied, which is but a way to say it is created. That creation story, a story that includes those creatures we call human beings, is a story that must be enacted. The story and its enactment are inseparable because the One who creates is a living God who would befriend and love God's creatures. This is a book of very personal testimonies about why or how that liturgical enactment of God's desire to have us as friends means we must learn how, as the stars do, to dance with the music of redemption.

Reading through the chapters of the book cannot help but make one impressed by the modesty displayed throughout these testimonies. Such modesty is appropriate because the writers have learned through the liturgy that they are not the center of the cosmos. But the modesty of those who have written could give the impression that the book is not all that important. But this book is more than it seems because if God through the liturgy did not produce lives like those that grace this book, then what we do as Christians when we worship God is false comfort in the face of what otherwise might appear to be the pointlessness of our death-determined lives.

That, moreover, is why, as many of these testimonies suggest, the liturgy is but an expression of the truth of the resurrection of Jesus from death. We worship a living God, which means that this really is the body and blood of our Savior. That realism, that undeniable reality, runs through these essays, which often describe how these folk discovered that they literally could not live without the life they were given through the liturgy. To be sure those liturgies were enacted by that confused and confusing church identified as "The Episcopal Church" but it is hard to avoid God showing up.

The chapters in this book should make one hopeful about that church, that is, The Episcopal Church. If The Episcopal Church has a magisterium it clearly must be the Book of Common Prayer. It is that book that helps Episcopalians discover they are joined to people across time and space. Indeed, as these essays exemplify, the liturgy in Spain, in forests, in churches of the poor, in small and large churches, and in countless other contexts are united by the common worship of God. That does not mean that the liturgy is or must be the same in every setting, but it does mean that we do things as Episcopalians that make it possible to recognize in vastly different contexts that we are worshiping the same God.

As many of these essays attest, moreover, the care the church provides in the face of challenges such as the everyday work of being a priest, what it means to grow old, the sustaining of marriage, the death of a child, and facing our death depends on the work of the liturgy. Without the liturgical enactment of the life of the One we believe is nothing less than the incarnation of the Father's love we would lack the means to know how to be present to one another, not only in times of crisis, but also when we are appropriately happy. At least that is the indelible impression the life-stories in this book leave. For it turns out, as these stories exemplify, we are not alone in the cosmos but in fact we are surrounded by a mighty cloud of fellow worshipers.

Paula, my wife, and I are communicants at the Episcopal Church of the Holy Family in Chapel Hill, North Carolina. Paula is a Methodist minister appointed by her bishop to Holy Family. Bishop Curry, then bishop of North Carolina and now the current bishop of North Carolina, Samuel Rodman, have given their blessing to that arrangement. Paula has a liturgical bearing that I find at once attractive and frightening. She really expects God to show up. I call attention to Paula's witness to join her (and my) story to the stories that make up this book because, as this book makes clear, through the sharing of such stories we discover our lives would make no sense without the truthful beauty of the liturgy.

Stanley Hauerwas

Acknowledgments

This project was conceived, developed, and completed in the context of worship. We served together at St. Anne's Episcopal Church in Annapolis, Maryland, where for nine years the bedrock of our ministries was the faithful and vibrant liturgical life of that parish. We currently serve as appointed missionaries of The Episcopal Church and are grateful to the Global Missions Office for their support and for sending us to the College of Transfiguration where we are visiting lecturers and participants in the dynamic worship life of this community. We are grateful to the members and staff of St. Anne's Parish, to Chuck Robertson, David Copley, and Elizabeth Boe of the Global Missions Office, and to the staff and students of the College of Transfiguration to whom this book is dedicated.

Introduction

There are several wonderful books about the theology and development of liturgy. This isn't one of them. In this book, we gather insights about worship by a number of people in The Episcopal Church who are bold enough to try to find language to describe how worship has formed them, surprised them, amazed them, comforted or confronted them; or rather, how God has done that through Episcopal liturgy.

We are priests, people who get asked the questions priests get asked: Why worship? Why at that time? In that place? With those words? Sometimes the questions are asked as challenges, other times in wonderment or bafflement, particularly by people who aren't as in the habit of showing up in church on Sundays as we are. These essays don't so much answer these questions as they name some truths, some longing, some Love we know we can't live without.

We originally envisioned this collection as focused on the experience of worship on Sundays, with the working title "Sunday Morning: Reflections on Episcopal Worship." Some authors, appropriately, ventured beyond Sundays, and the book is all the richer for it. Hence the title *Common Prayer*.

In these pages, Spencer Reece dresses for his little entrance; Rhonda Mawhood Lee falls in love with Jesus by flashlight; Neil Alexander confesses that he is a Sunday-keeper; Sophfronia Scott gets a taste of grace; Lauren Winner wonders what the deal is with communion wafers; Rodney Clapp plays on Sundays; Melissa

Deckman Fallon worries she is a bad Episcopalian; Steve Fowl provides a view from the choir; Amy Richter believes in demons; Cameron Dezen Hammon wants to belong to something; Duane Miller sweats in the *calid* Spanish summer; Paul Fromberg dances in friendship with God; Michael Battle ponders Zen-like riddles and bubble gum-blowing acolytes; BJ Heyboer finds a home at the foot of the cross; Ian Markham tries to be an atheist but fails; Kim Edwards realizes there is no such thing as ordinary time; Luisa Bonillas crosses the US-Mexico border every Sunday to go to church; worship saves Joe Pagano's marriage; Kathryn Greene-McCreight smears ashes on her children's foreheads; C. K. Robertson blesses heroes; Batman, Robin, and Supergirl show up for the blessing of Amy Peterson's home; Rachel Marie Stone longs to bring her pets with her everywhere, including church; and Fred Bahnson recounts the legendary chainsaw Eucharist.

We asked this group of writers to engage in an exercise of theological memoir, to write in their own strong, distinct voices about their experiences of Episcopal worship. We were both thrilled with and awed by the result: personal essays that are funny, vulnerable, faithful; people telling of loss, joy, play, belonging, love. This way of writing is risky. But so is engaging whole-heartedly in worship. These authors show us that this way of writing, this way of worshiping, this way of living is worth it. They share their flesh and blood lives with us and we meet the God who meets us in worship. This shouldn't surprise us. In worship, Jesus shares his flesh and blood life with us; he pours himself out so we may have life and have life more abundantly.

Through the particularity of their reflections on life and worship, we don't just get to know the authors. There are twenty-three authors in this collection, but the main character who emerges is the God we know in Jesus Christ, the God of, as Steve Fowl puts it, "unrelenting and eager openness." This book is an invitation to risk offering the particularities of your own life in the worship of the same God.

1

The Little Entrance

SPENCER REECE

I live in the center of Madrid, built in the center of Spain by
the order of a king around 1606. I live on the top floor of the
Spanish Episcopal Cathedral *in the center of the center.* Put your
thumb on a Spanish map. Put it in the center of Madrid. I'm right
under that. I've been here seven years and when I ask my boss, the
Episcopal bishop of Spain, how long I will be here, he says it is a
contracto indefinito.

No one is more surprised than me that I am here. Spaniards
perhaps think the strange expression on my face is the result of

all my labored "r" rolling, but it is probably also the fact of my wonder. The place and its people suit me, although they are a place and a people that couldn't be more different from me, and perhaps that is *why* they suit me.

I am the national secretary for the Episcopal bishop. As the Anglican church spread through the British Empire in the nineteenth century, it mainly took root in English-speaking places—British colonies, including the United States, where, largely because of the revolution there, it decided to call itself Episcopal rather than Anglican. But somehow the Anglican Church also took hold here in Spain, embraced by the Spaniards, *in* Spanish. Unlikely. There was an effort to spread the Anglican faith into Portugal and Italy too, but Spain was where it caught most. We're so tiny and curious here in Catholic Spain—five thousand believers in a country of 43 million Catholics—that Spaniards are always astonished at our existence no matter how many times I explain it.

I help the bishop with every manner of thing in Spanish and in English: I answer the door, I do the church newsletter, I answer the phone, I travel with him, I conduct services, I preach, I empty trash, I hand out bags of food on Saturday. In between all of that, I have time in this office to look at the map of Spain with tiny pins showing where our few priests are.

Several minutes past nine in the morning. Madrid wakes up. Children in the tiny street lined with four-story nineteenth-century brick buildings head to school. Their yearning yelps echo and increase as the sounds bounce off the building walls, entering my small living room, where I put down my cup of coffee. I am dressed in a faded black shirt and black dress pants left over from the days when I worked at Brooks Brothers. My plastic white collar is in my hand, I shake it like a soldier with a bandage ready to attend to the wounded. Around my neck swings a huge set of keys. I jangle when I move so I always sound like the coins the homeless shake in their paper cups.

Oh this crumbling cathedral with buckling windows, cracked window glass, chipping paint, and sewage that backs up under the office! This tiny twig of the church that was founded for Spanish Anglicans and closed during the dictatorship. The whole place smells like an old book that has been in a dank basement for forty years.

I come down my four flights of burnished wooden steps with iron railings. The bishop is surely in his pew. I'm late, but it's Spain, so this is nothing. I enter the sacristy. I don my full-length cassock. I fasten the black buttons at the top. I cinch the black fabric belt around my waist with the fringe ends. I look quickly in the spotted mirror next to the cheap broken plastic clock where time is always stopped. I pull on my giant white surplice that billows like a parachute, then a tippet, a black scarf for morning prayer, which I kiss in the center as I was taught to do before it goes around my neck. Something about the idea of wearing a uniform appeals to me. A uniform for a profession that George Herbert said was characterized by love: he wrote in *The Country Parson* that "love was the business and the aim" for parsons. The uniform advertises that. What a magical thing to have a uniform that signals love.

In my hand I have the tattered program for morning prayer, the white paper browned by the dirty fingers of the poor who have fingered these pages for years waiting for their bags of food on Saturday evenings. Finally, I snap my white plastic collar in place behind my head. I turn the latch that goes into the cathedral. I begin morning prayer for two—three if the bishop's wife joins us. The bishop stands for my entrance. I go in a straight line toward the Bible I will read from, ready for love.

Opening up the Bible and finding the passage on the rota, I begin. In the Greek Orthodox Church, this moment when the priest opens the Bible and reads from it is called "the little entrance." I like that term, the image of a priest popping out from behind a reredos as out of some kind of religious dollhouse. I do this every week. I smooth the tissue-thin Bible pages, clear my throat, and read.

2

Indissoluble

RHONDA MAWHOOD LEE

I stepped out of the cool darkness of the Catholic Cathedral of St. John the Baptist into the August warmth of its flagstone courtyard. Set high on a hill, the cathedral watched over the town of Fira on the Greek island of Santorini; looking back over my shoulder I saw the bay below sparkling as the sun strolled at a summer pace toward the western horizon. The Mass I had just left was my first in a decade. Out of respect for Catholic practice, I hadn't taken Communion, but even so, the liturgy had left me as peaceful and satisfied as an indulgent meal with friends. I knew my husband would be waiting on the patio of our hotel room on Fira's main plaza with the souvlaki and wine he had promised to buy while I was at church. We would savor them along with a final sunset before leaving the island tomorrow.

As I turned my attention from the bay back to the courtyard, he appeared. Not my husband; Jesus. He fell into step beside me, turned his head so his warm brown eyes met my green ones, and smiled. His message sounded as loudly in my head as if he had actually spoken the words: "*Now* will you admit you're one of mine?" Not out loud, I wouldn't; we were surrounded by pedestrians and I didn't want to appear insane. But the seeds of peace the Mass had planted bloomed into joy, and I gave Jesus a smile and just the tiniest of nods. He nodded back. Then he was gone.

Our reunion had been a long time coming.

A school night, twenty-five years earlier: I was eight years old, propped on my pillow, bedclothes tented over my head, a flashlight illuminating the tiny print on the thin page resting on my lap. I had fallen so deep into the story I didn't hear my mother calling. The pressure of her hand on my shoulder through the covers made me jump.

"Rhonda, it's late. Put the book away and go to sleep."

I considered pretending already to be asleep, but there was no way to sell that ruse at such close quarters. So I snapped off the light. "Okay. Good night."

"Good night, dear."

Sometimes, I would hear my mother's footsteps coming down the hall and switch off the light before hearing her pause in my doorway and turn away without saying a word. Other times, I would fall asleep in the middle of a page, wake up past midnight in my dark room, and realize my mother had silently extinguished the flashlight on her way to bed.

The book that had me so enthralled was one she would have preferred I not open. But she had never forbidden me to read anything that caught my eye and this, at least, was a classic. She hoped my infatuation with the protagonist was a phase, but to me, it was love.

And he took the seven loaves and the fishes, and gave thanks, and brake them, and gave to his disciples, and the disciples to the multitude.

And Jesus rebuked the devil; and he departed out of him: and the child was cured from that very hour.

And he took the damsel by the hand, and said unto her, Talitha cumi; which is, being interpreted, Damsel, I say unto thee, arise.

He fed people, healed them, and even raised them from the dead—or brought them to their feet when they and everyone around them thought they were done for, which for me amounted to the same thing. I wanted everything Jesus offered.

But my mother was dead set against me seeing him. Never mind that she had promised to raise me as a member of his family. In January of 1967, when my mother dressed my infant self in a borrowed baptismal gown trimmed with lace, then wrapped me in a white shawl against Montréal's winter winds, she had other broken vows on her mind. She was a twenty-three-year-old newly single mother whose marriage had fallen apart the previous summer, halfway through her pregnancy. Her husband, my biological father, had skipped town never to be heard from again, so my mother had moved back in with her parents. As a young working-class woman struggling to support the two of us, she needed her family's support, and her Presbyterian Scottish immigrant mother required that I be "christened." It had been years since my mother had entered the church of her childhood. Something, somewhere along the way—she never said what, and she never said when—had broken whatever bond she may have felt with God and the people who claimed to be God's. Now, rebellion was a luxury she couldn't afford, but no one could make her take the ritual seriously.

Nothing changed when my mother married her second husband, the only father I ever knew. They had gotten together in the late 1960s and married in the 1970s, when the question of whether or not our province, Québec, would declare independence from

Canada dominated the news and divided families. My mother's clan and his Catholic, French-speaking kin found it equally hard to accept their union, but in time, the fact that he claimed me as his own helped win over both sides. They married in the Unitarian Church, the only one that would bless the union of a divorced, lapsed Presbyterian and a divorced Catholic and spare them the mountain of paperwork a civil marriage in Québec required.

Religion highlighted the fault lines running through our family, setting off clear boundaries for us to tiptoe around. My parents managed their differences by agreeing that faith, as they often repeated, was "private." So private, it was bad manners to talk about it. Every Saturday afternoon just before five, my father would leave for Mass without a word of good-bye, returning in time for dinner, and every week, my mother stayed home. Two or three times a year, I was allowed to tag along. I loved everything about church: the beeswax-and-spice fragrance; the spotlights illuminating the altar in the otherwise dim space; the brightly colored windows; the priest's utter focus as he consecrated the bread and wine; the sense that somehow, in that moment, we were connected to the Jesus I knew from my bedtime reading. When I heard, *On the night before he died for us, our Lord Jesus Christ took bread; and when he had given thanks, he broke it, and gave it to his disciples, and said, "Take, eat . . ."* I remembered, *And he took the cup, and gave thanks, and said, Take this, and divide it among yourselves: For I say unto you, I will not drink of the fruit of the vine until the kingdom of God shall come.*

I wasn't sure what, exactly, the kingdom of God was, but clearly, church was the place to plunge more deeply into the story that kept me up late night after night. I knew my mother wouldn't agree to me attending Mass regularly, so I kept my eyes open for alternatives. Out running errands on Saturday mornings, I would point to Presbyterian or United churches and suggest in the most casual tone I could manage, "I could go there tomorrow. You could drop me off." Sometimes she would answer, "I don't think so, dear"; other times, "We'll see."

One evening when I was about eleven, while my mother was bending over the oven to check the progress of a roast chicken and I was shredding lettuce for salad, I asked, "Did Jesus really come back to life?" (My father was the practicing Christian in our house, but I saved the big questions for my mother.) She pulled out the chicken, set it down, took off her oven mitts. The only sound was ripping romaine. Then finally, "I don't think so, dear."

Pretty soon, I put away the Bible and gave up my quiet crusade. As I moved from childhood to adolescence, I still regularly fell asleep with the sheets over my head. But I wasn't falling into Jesus's world anymore. Now I ducked to protect myself from the world collapsing around me. My mother's long struggle with depression turned deadly, as she tried to kill herself when I was twelve, thirteen, and fourteen; my grandparents retired back to Scotland months after that last attempt; my father silently stopped going to church and took up a campaign, unsuccessful but tenacious, to drown his anxiety and helplessness in beer. Believing in resurrection seemed too much like trusting adults to protect me: a hope that was sure to disappoint.

At twenty-eight, I stood in my mother's kitchen looking out at white lawns, skeletal trees, and icy streets edged with exhaust-stained black snow. Where I'm from, February's only virtue is its short length: four weeks to cross off between January's deep freeze and the thaws of late March or April. But in my family's emotional calendar, February stretched endlessly: the month in which my mother often threatened or attempted suicide and when, a couple of days earlier, just after her fifty-second birthday, she had finally killed herself.

She had been widowed five years, by cancer that might not have been fatal if my father's anxiety hadn't kept him from the doctor so long. I had moved to North Carolina for graduate school a couple of years later, tired of waiting for my mother to acknowledge she had a treatable mental illness, tired of molding my life around her death threats. Now, as I prepared to plan her funeral at the table where she had written her goodbye note, it dawned on me that I was on my own: an only child, unmarried, both parents dead. Within weeks, I would have buried my mother and disposed of her belongings. Then, I thought, "I can do whatever I want."

The next thought arrived instantaneously: "I can go to church."

"I can buy a motorcycle" or "I can go tend bar in the Bahamas" would have shocked me less. But then, the past few days had been full of shocks. I put "going to church" at the end of my long list of things to think about later.

That July, in the middle of the lush, humid, Southern summer, I bought two dresses I hoped were suitable for Sundays, looked up the service times of the local Unitarian fellowship, and found my way there.

Gifts the Unitarian Church gave me in our three years together:

- A place to sit and sob through hymns, only one of which I knew ("Amazing Grace," my grandmother's favorite), for a year;

- New habits: organizing my weekends around Sunday mornings and paying my pledge right after my rent;

- A ministry on the pastoral care team, when I was ready for it after my year of tears;

- The possibility of a new vocation, as the community began to ask if I had considered ordination.

What it couldn't give me:

- Jesus.

I blamed fundamentalists, and the political damage they inflicted on my adopted home, for ruining the Christian church for me. I had joined the Unitarians because they had welcomed my parents, and because they seemed like anti-fundamentalists. But after three years in a kind yet resolutely rationalist community, I started to wonder again: what about the resurrection? Could Jesus really have come back to life?

An unvoiced desire that might have sounded like hope led me, on a Greek vacation in 1999, to follow my father's long-abandoned footsteps to Saturday evening Mass. Jesus met me there.

Back from vacation, I went looking for him in The Episcopal Church. Its Eucharist was essentially the same as the Mass that had enthralled me as a child, but it ordained women. It might become home.

My first Sunday, I stood with the rest of the congregation to say the Nicene Creed, turning over its statements in my mind, wondering, "Do I believe that?" as my mouth pronounced the words on the page. I knelt to pray a whole-hearted confession—my first ever, to God—and exhaled a long breath as the priest pronounced absolution.

Then, as he prepared to consecrate the bread and wine, I wondered, should I take Communion? The bulletin said "all baptized Christians" were welcome to. I was baptized, but was I a Christian? What were the criteria?

Maybe the Book of Common Prayer could help. Flipping to page 299, "Holy Baptism," my eye fell on the notes "Concerning the Service." The first two lines settled my internal debate: "Holy Baptism is full initiation by water and the Holy Spirit into Christ's Body the Church. The bond which God establishes in Baptism is indissoluble."

Indissoluble. It didn't matter that my parents and godparents hadn't brought me up in the church. It didn't matter how long it had taken me to return to the Eucharist, or that Jesus had had to appear beside me on a Greek island to get my attention. God himself had made me a member of Christ's body, and no one could amputate me from it.

So I got up and took Communion. And I kept going back, week after week, to the altar rail, to Bible study, to the church's community kitchen, to conversations and prayers in the parking lot and hospital rooms and at dinner tables. My childhood intuition had been correct: church was the portal to Jesus and the world he opened up. My parents, in their shared fear that religious conflict would tear apart their fragile entente, had been wrong. Faith wasn't private. But it was deeply personal, as personal as a lover pursuing me halfway around the world.

My relationship with that Lover can only flourish in the community that keeps meeting at the altar to re-tell the story that is his and, because we are his, ours too; that laid hands on me at my confirmation and again at my ordinations; that will, I hope, gather around me as I pass from this life to the next. When that moment comes, my fellow members of Jesus Christ's body will remind me that I am dying as I finally learned to live: in sure and certain hope of the resurrection.

3

Of Sacraments and Sundays

J. NEIL ALEXANDER

Years ago I was called to the hospital to be present with a young couple whose child was gravely ill at the time of birth. By the time I reached the hospital the child had died and when I entered the room the young parents, distressed and deeply grieving, were cuddling the motionless corpse of their long-desired baby. As a priest and pastor I had never been in quite this situation before. In the torture of the moment, I dredged up from the residue of seminary that, in such moments, it was not unknown for a priest to baptize a child that died at birth as a means to comfort and console the devastated parents. Perhaps, it was hoped, they could find solace in the fact that their child had a name and had been claimed by a loving and merciful God in holy baptism. Later pastoral experience would give some credence to this theory even if it remains sacramentally awkward and theologically untenable.

On this particular occasion, however, things took a different turn. When the right moment seemed to arrive, I asked the young couple, still gently rocking their lifeless baby, if they wanted me to baptize the child. Much to my surprise, the young father looked at me, tears streaming down his face, and said, "No, that will not be necessary. Baptism is for this life and our child is not going to have a 'this life.'" He then looked at his wife who nodded her consent and affirmed what he had said. Few moments in my pastoral ministry have had such a lasting impact on me. Few encounters have helped me see more clearly the role of sacraments in the living of our lives.

I fear we sometimes imagine that baptism is like fire insurance. We do this to ward off something else happening or, if it does, the baptized are somehow protected. It is as though baptism is some sort of watery prophylaxis. We discover that folks often want their baby "done," baptized, because of some lingering superstition about a God who needs to be placated in order for grace and mercy to be realized. Or, it may simply grow out of a need to maintain social conventions and family tradition, thus making happy the older generations of the family. What is missing in both cases is any sense of what baptism is for and why the young couple in the process of letting go of the precious child saw no need for their child to be baptized. This points, I believe, to why sacraments and Sundays are so critical to our formation as the body of Christ.

More on sacraments a bit later on, but for the moment, let's consider the importance of Sunday in our formation as the people of God. One of the things that delights me most about being an Episcopalian is the 1979 Book of Common Prayer and its rather stunning clarity about the primacy of Sunday in our common life. We celebrate the various seasons of the church's year of grace, we keep the daily offices of psalmody, Scripture, and prayer, and our sanctoral calendar overflows with lesser feasts and fasts. Sunday, however, is the taproot from which everything else is nourished and given its life. Sunday-keeping is the defining aspect of our public identity.

All of this is the case, of course, because the event that gives us our identity as Jesus-followers more clearly than any other, not exclusively but more clearly, took place *on the first day of the week.* Resurrection is not the only aspect of the Jesus-story that shapes our identity, but it is *the divine action* without which the rest of the story ceases to be very compelling. Consequently, for Jesus-followers the primary act of Sunday is to gather as a community and give public witness to his death and resurrection. Even when the lectionary calls our attention to other aspects of the life of Jesus, his actions or his teaching, it is still placed before us on Sunday in the course of a eucharistic rite that has no theme other than the anamnesis of Jesus's death and resurrection. It is for this reason that the fundamental rhythm of Christian life is a weekly one, just as it is for our Jewish friends who find so much of their identity in weekly Sabbath-keeping. No other aspect of practicing of the faith of the church shapes us as Jesus-followers quite as clearly as the relentlessness of Sunday, week after week, for a lifetime. No other activity of Christians—gathering publicly on Sunday for word and sacrament—more clearly reveals to the world the primacy of resurrection as the source of our identity.

What happens on Sunday, therefore, is of enormous consequence for our formation as Jesus-followers. The Sunday assembly of the faithful is the principal time and place where the Word of God—Jesus, the Risen One—is raised up in both proclamation and preaching and in the sacraments of baptism and Eucharist. This does not mean that our engagement with the Word of God is in any way limited to the Sunday assembly. Bible reading and prayer and serious Scripture study, alone or with others, are powerful ways of deepening our faith and understanding. Theological study and reflection on the sacraments of the resurrection are also of profound importance. But all caveats aside, the church of Jesus through the centuries has acknowledged the primacy of the

Sunday assembly as *the time and place* for word and sacrament. Preaching Christ crucified and risen enjoys a particularly poignant *habitus* on Sunday, not only on Easter Day and the Sundays of the Great Fifty Days, but on *every* Sunday. Even amidst the terror of Advent, or the wilderness experience of Lent, the brilliant light of the Sunday of the Transfiguration, or a hot summer Sunday with only a few sayings or a short parable on offer, we are always drawn to see every bit of it in some sort of relationship to death and resurrection. That does not mean we find Jesus under every rock in the Hebrew Scriptures, or that every story of Jesus in the New Testament is told to make a point about death and resurrection. What it does mean is that when we proclaim the stories that shape us, we do so premierly on a Sunday—the day of resurrection—and thus we cannot escape hearing and experiencing everything in light of our of weekly public witness to death and resurrection. It simply makes us who we are.

From time to time this will create a sense of dissonance in the liturgy. I remember, for example, a Christmas many years ago when a relatively new member of the church harangued me for the fact that our celebration of the birth of Jesus was a Eucharist. In her mind, the Eucharist was lodged in the narratives of Holy Week, particularly Maundy Thursday and Good Friday, and her holy imagination was stuck permanently in the upper room. Because it was Christmas our thoughts should turn to the pastoral hillsides near Bethlehem, bleating sheep, lowing cattle, and wonder-struck shepherds. To interrupt the placidity of the moment with death and resurrection was just too much. But that's the point. Such tension—dissonance—as arresting as it may seem at first, is precisely the place wherein we find our bearings as followers of the crucified-and-risen Jesus. We seek to release that tension, or muffle that dissonance, at the peril of the richness of our faith and discipleship. The cross and resurrection cast a long shadow over the whole of the Jesus-story, over the story of the church, and over the times and places of our own stories. The uneasiness we sometimes feel in such moments is likely to be the indication that the Holy Spirit is powerfully at work within us. It is this pervasive sense of the Word of God—Jesus, the Risen One—that is fully present in the Sunday assembly as we praise, proclaim, preach, and pray. It is the Word of God—Jesus, the Risen One—that is made known to us in the sacraments of the resurrection: baptism and Eucharist.

When we speak of the sacraments of the resurrection, what do we mean? There are, of course, many explanations of the sacraments and of a sacramental life. Most of them are valuable for our reflection and deepen our understanding of how God is manifest in those means of grace we call sacraments, particularly baptism and Eucharist. The fact that the tradition often refers to the sacraments as holy mysteries should be a clue that we will never fully fathom their depth and meaning, nor will we ever fully grasp what God does in, for, and through us by means of them. Here, however, I want to invite you to think of sacraments, in the first place, as gifts.

A gift, if it is truly that, is, well, a *gift*. It is free. Perhaps hoped for, but still unearned and unexpected. It demands nothing in return. That's not to say, of course, that a gracious and loving response to the gift is not appropriate—a sincere thank you, perhaps—but if there are strings attached, it is no longer a gift. A gift with strings attached is a transaction, not a gift. Sacraments are gifts.

Take infant baptism, for example. There are not many living creatures that are as helpless at the time of their birth as a human infant. As every parent knows all too well, a newborn requires *everything, absolutely everything* to be done for it! It has to be fed at the mother's breast. It has to be changed by a loving father. It has to be entertained by an older sibling. Whatever the shape of the family that welcomes the child, and there are many, everyone is going to get into the act. Everything it needs must be provided by someone else. What's more, the child has no capacity to earn any of this care and attention.

The child also has to be carried to the font. What happens in the sacrament of baptism is something that this helpless hunk of flesh cannot ask for, prepare for, or earn in any way. It comes to the child as a totally free, unencumbered, unmerited, unfettered gift of love and grace. As the child grows up, there will be all manner of questions about word and water, smelly oils, and hand-laying by people who sometimes wear pointy hats. There will be talk of creeds and covenants, responses and responsibilities. Some priest is likely to come along and insert a word like "regeneration" into the kid's vocabulary and talk about what it means to be born again, or from above, or from some place or another that is close to the heart of God. But before it is any of that, baptism is a gift, plain and simple.

One of my teachers used to say that life in Christ is mostly about surviving your baptism. It is about coming to terms with the radicality of the grace of God. It is about facing the fact that you really are loved beyond your wildest imagination. It is about being held in the arms of a lover who will never let you go. Baptism is sort of like a lifeline that is always there, always within arm's reach. Baptism gives us something to grab on to for dear life when we've lost our moorings, lost our courage, or lost our minds. It is there to keep us going when broken hearts, or broken promises, or broken bodies, make everything a chore. It is there to cling to when we have exhausted every other possibility. Baptism is God's gift to us for the living of these days, for this life. God doesn't need baptism. We do. It is God's way of keeping us close. The young couple with a dead child had no need to have their baby baptized because baptism is for this life. They knew that their little one was known to God in the mother's womb. The child was God's beloved long before the baby was theirs. And they also knew that their own baptisms—into the death and resurrection of Jesus—were the lifelines they were going to need to grab hold of through all of the grief and agony that was to come. Healing would come also, as it so often does, in the waters of their own baptisms, stirred by the Spirit, rushing with grace, brimming with mercy, and overflowing with love.

Where does one learn this sort of thing? There are many paths to understanding. One can listen to the experience of others, or contemplate the role of sacraments in one's own life, or perhaps read a theological reflection like the one before you. But what is the path to the embodiment of the centrality of word and sacraments in our lives? How do we capture the richness of a sacramental life with the whole of our being and not simply as an act of assent to an idea? Embodiment comes, I believe, from the disciplined participation in the public, weekly Sunday assembly where the Word of God—Jesus, the Risen One—and the Sacraments of the Resurrection are raised up, celebrated, and received, without hesitation or apology.

Like baptism, Holy Communion is also, first and foremost, a gift. There are libraries full of books, written through the centuries, about the celebration of the Holy Eucharist and the meaning and benefits of Holy Communion. The perspectives are broad and deep. The explanations that are foreign to our experience, or contrary to our own understandings, still have much to teach us. It is easy to get caught up in the nature of the bread or the alcohol content of the wine. We are also quick to obsess over the shelf life of the real presence and wear ourselves out about how Jesus gets into the bread, how long he stays, and how he gets out of it. These, and many more, are not unimportant theological questions. There is no argument here that we should not engage them fully. But as I noted above with respect to baptism, the first order of things is to embrace Holy Communion as a gift.

So, what is the gift of Communion? Fortunately, this question has many answers. I mean, really, who wants a diamond with only one facet? Some will suggest that the forgiveness of sins is the gift of Communion. "Broken and shed *for you* for the forgiveness of sins." And, so it is. Others might say that the gift of Communion is "bread for the wilderness and wine for the journey." Surviving your baptism requires sustenance. True enough. Another might suggest that the gift of Communion is food. We feed those we love, and Holy Communion is God feeding us because God loves us. Seems reasonable. There is nothing patently wrong with any of these explanations and there are many, many more like them. Such is the richness of the gift of Communion.

I believe that different facets of the gift of Communion appeal to us at different times in our lives as we take this journey ever more deeply into the mystery of Christ. Each of the ones above, and several others, have had a particular appeal to me at earlier times in my life. At the present time, however, I believe that when I receive the gift of Communion, I am taking into myself, my soul and body, the risen life of Jesus. The Risen One gives himself to me, not just theoretically, but sacramentally. I feed upon the fullness of his risen life and it nourishes both soul and body. It is not for me commemorative, but generative. It makes me me, in Christ. When I meditate on the gift of Communion at this stage of life, I give thanks (eucharist!) that in holy baptism I became a part of the risen body of Christ and that in Holy Communion a part of the risen body of Christ, sacramentally, becomes a part of me.

And lest I forget, where did I learn this? In a library? In a classroom? From a priest? Well, sort of. Each contributed. But I learned this mostly on countless Sunday mornings when the baptized of God assembled to make their weekly public witness to the death and resurrection of Jesus. For me, understanding comes from lots of sources. Embodiment comes from the lifetime discipline of Sunday assembly in the power of resurrection.

It seems almost commonplace these days for people to excuse themselves from the Sunday assembly on the argument that they are "spiritual, but not religious." I certainly want to honor the journey such folks are on and I make no judgment against them. That said, I simply don't get it. I am not wired that way. I am pretty much the reverse: I am religious, but not spiritual. Never have been. I don't expect I ever will be. The fact that I find a good advertisement for Nike running shoes to be a highly theological message tells you all you need to know: *just do it!* Don't overthink it. Don't wrap it too tightly around the axle of your emotions. Just lace them up and go! (to a Sunday assembly near you where the Risen Christ and resurrection sacraments are the agenda).

Perhaps now you are beginning to see why The Episcopal Church and our life of common prayer is so important to me. I grew up in a practicing family. My very earliest memories took place in church. I realized as a young child that music, perhaps as much as anything else, carries the faith and shapes the soul. I remember coming to the realization that good preaching had a positive impact on me even when I wasn't sure of its every detail. I was wowed by the sacraments. There's really no other way to put it. All this is important to me for one reason: I am not, nor will I ever be, a good enough Christian to survive without word and sacrament. I honor those who can go to a church that is mostly singing and preaching, but I am pretty sure if that's all there was to it, I would have left the faith long ago. If I went to a church where baptism is merely the marker of "saying yes" to Jesus, I would live in fear and despair that it was never enough, and still more anxiously, that I am never enough. I need to be in a church that reminds me every Sunday that in the Spirit-filled waters of holy baptism, God in Jesus said "yes!" to me, and *that's enough*. If I went to a church that had Holy Communion only on rare occasions and did so only because they had not figured out a way around "do this," I would starve to death. I require a regular diet of the Risen One, especially on Sundays.

There will always be those who want quick results and instant gratification even with respect to their life in Christ. Such good folk will always find The Episcopal Church frustrating and it will be difficult for them to find a comfortable home among us. Many of us, however, are Episcopalians because we are wired for the long haul: a journey from the font to eternity that is punctuated by a thousand successive Sundays that carry us forward by the inexhaustible energy of resurrection.

4

A Taste of Grace

SOPHFRONIA SCOTT

On this Sunday morning I've already changed shirts three times. I can't figure out what would be comfortable in church on a hot summer day. At least one top I discard because I've remembered I'm serving as a chalice minister and the shirt's collar would interfere with fastening the top button of the long black cassock I'll wear underneath a white cotta. It takes me a few more minutes to figure out it doesn't matter what I wear because I will be sweltering in the cassock and cotta. A T-shirt will suffice.

Nothing about this morning is going well. My teenage son performed in a musical the night before and went to bed late. He's tired and dragging his feet. My husband's irritation with his slowness has them sniping at each other. I would be content to leave them both at home. My son is supposed to be the crucifer at this service and I even offer to stand in for him because I'm trained in all the acolyte duties. My husband rightfully points out that he has to learn to do what he's engaged to do, even when tired. This doesn't make the situation any better.

I want to yell at them to cut it out, but I don't. Instead I absorb the energy and let it go bounding through my system on a kind of whitewater rafting trip. To be honest, my annoyance is not really with them. It's from the feeling I have as we walk across the church parking lot that today will not be the day.

It's a day I've been seeking since the beginning of the year, when my service on our church's vestry concluded. For the first time in several years I'm not teaching a class or holding a meeting or setting up a table of muffins, coffee, or sign-up sheets. I'd skirted on the edge of burnout, my toes on the crown of a volcano. I knew if I weren't careful I would fall into the abyss and not return to church. There were days when I couldn't finish setting up for class or a program before the service so the best I could do was try to be done before communion. I'd enter the sanctuary from the rear, go to the rail and take communion, then leave the sanctuary and go back to my work. And even if I was done setting up before the service, I'd still be thinking about whether I had enough handouts, my opening and closing prayers, what I would say during announcements to get people to attend, or, if I were teaching Sunday school, whether I could get the students interested and talking about the material.

I was not thinking about worship. Once upon a time I did. When my family and I first starting going to church and joined the Episcopal faith in 2011, I used to spend the liturgy sitting quietly in the pew, a small prayer journal in my lap, so I could write down inklings of what I felt God wanted me to focus on for the coming week.[1] I would wait for the words that set me on fire. Or, at the very least, give me a new set of eyes through which to view the world and my place in God's creation. I miss that sense of simplicity. It's

---

1. I share this journey in the book *This Child of Faith: Raising a Spiritual Child in a Secular World* (Brewster, MA: Paraclete, 2018).

been eight months and, aside from occasionally serving at the altar, I am sitting quietly in a pew again and it's not the same. Something has complicated my spiritual thinking and it's like I'm wrestling with a dragon. Can I ever get back to that sense of peace, I wonder. Am I supposed to?

Strangely enough, it is this feeling that I fear will eventually keep me from returning each week, not the fear of burnout. At some point my son, having forgotten that it was his idea all those years ago to come to church, will ask, as teens tend to do, why we go to church. I want to have an answer for him and for myself as well. I keep showing up because I think what I've lost must be here somewhere, as though it's in the lost-and-found box in the fellowship room. But I don't know what I'm looking for other than this desire to take hold of my faith so I can feel it in both hands.

On the bulletin board outside our rector's office is a set of words: Love, Faith, Self-Control, Humility, Peace, Patience, Confidence, Kindness, Hope. Pieces of Scripture, printed on small white rectangles of card stock, fill envelope pockets below each word. The center of the bulletin board says, "Take what you need." This morning I need patience so I pull a card from the envelope as my son and I walk past the board on our way to the vesting room. It quotes Lamentations 3:25–27:

> The Lord is good to everyone
> who trusts in him,
> So it is best for us to wait in patience—
> to wait for him to save us—
> And it is best to learn this
> patience in our youth.[2]

Okay, it's not quite what I need to hear—I'm not even sure what I need to hear—but I'll hang onto the thought. I put the card in my purse.

Two unexpected encounters ensue. One of the ushers is someone who had served with me on the vestry and I haven't seen him in a long time. We share an affectionate hug. Then, as my son

2. GNB.

and I stand in the back of the sanctuary waiting for the service to begin, I notice a little girl, around four years old, staring at me. She could be doing this for any reason, but I'm guessing she's looking at my hair. I'm wearing my dreadlocks tied up and off my neck, but a few strays hang down my back. There are many days, and this is one of them, when I'm the only black person in the room so I'm used to receiving looks of curiosity. I wave at the child and she smiles and waves back. Are these inklings of the divine—a hug I didn't know I needed, the eyes of this little girl on me?

Our rector, Jenny, has been away and in her welcome message before the service she talks briefly about how during her travels she had attended a worship service on a beach. I feel a touch of envy. That would be something, to feel God's presence with my toes dug into sand or even seawater, and sending words of praise into salty air. I feel a familiar push and pull inside me—the tension between desire and sadness. The desire is the urge to sense God closely. The sadness is when it feels impossible to do so. In this moment it's the desire to be on a beach and have the direct sensation of God on my skin while at the same time knowing I can feel nothing but the slightly scratchy fabric of the dark cassock and the crisp white cotta.

The first reading is from 1 Kings 19:4–8, in which Elijah seems ready to give up the ghost, but suddenly there is a jar of water and a cake baked on hot stones. The angel tells him, "Get up and eat, otherwise, the journey will be too much for you." I think about sustenance. Am I starving? Is there something too sterile about my vestments and surroundings? Have I grown weary in a way that makes my journey back into connecting with worship too long and too hard? I'm still wondering if I should be outside somewhere, and I don't mean the outdoor service we will hold soon in a nearby park under a pavilion. I mean some place less tamed, where I sense the wind as an embrace or a shawl wrapped in love around my shoulders.

We read in unison the first eight verses of Psalm 34, ending with the line *Taste and see that the LORD is good.* The words turn over again and again in my mind while I'm still savoring the thought of Elijah's cake baked on hot stones. I know this cake was probably something akin to bread but I have cake on the brain because I love, and have since childhood, eating cake straight from the oven. I will even microwave a piece of cake to return it to that state of warmth before eating it. There is delight and comfort when a morsel touches the tongue in the right way and the flavor itself is a revelation. I think that must be what it is to taste the Lord.

The Gospel reading is from John and includes the lines *I am the bread of life. Whoever comes to me will never be hungry* . . . . I'm guessing the thoughts around eating and hunger connect to the sense in which something solid is taken into our physical being. Otherwise the words in the psalm would be "look and see," not *taste and see*. Something has to be taken in, ingested. And then, as Christ says, we will never be hungry. How does that work when I feel empty? When I can't quite find the sense of being filled or what might give that to me? But then there's the place in Mark where Christ talks about how, in terms of defilement, there's more reason to fear what comes from within than what comes from without. Is it the same for inspiration? Something must feed me from within?

Jenny begins her sermon by talking about when she baked bread as a young mother. She describes the warmth and the smells and the magic of working with the dough and the satisfying nature of the finished loaf. My husband is fond of making bread, though at this moment he hasn't done so in months. I can eat it all day and not care about the carb count. My son loves it too.

This makes me think of the Communion to come, and how a warm, substantial loaf of bread compares with our usual thin wafers pressed and stamped with a cross. The wafer would stick dryly to the roof of my mouth until the sip of wine released it. Again I feel that push-pull of desire and sadness. The wafers now seem too simple and sterile, but instead of going down the path of feeling there will be no connection for me in that wafer today, I summon my obedience and arrange my thinking to the point where I am willing to be fed this way, with the wafer. And though

25

I've managed this, it feels like a compromise, like everything has to be less. I have to be content with worship as is—I may never find the same sense of peace and Sabbath again; not having the right piece of Scripture when I need it; dealing as I grow older with increasing levels of loss as friends die and habits and traditions fall away. I must accept it as the way of the world.

Over the course of the service I am resigning myself to all this. I remind myself to just keep going with Julian of Norwich's words in my head that all shall be well. All manner of things shall be well. I am giving in as we move through the end of Jenny's sermon, the Nicene Creed, the Prayers of the People, the Confession of Sin, and the Peace.

When we begin the Offertory my eyes are on my hymnal. I don't watch the elements brought forth. It is only when I put the book down and come to the table for the Great Thanksgiving that I see a simple cloth covering a small mound on the altar. It's not the usual silver ciborium filled with wafers. My eyes flit over to the credence table to see if it's been forgotten. I'm already thinking how to signal my son on the other end of the altar that he has to go find it. Then Jenny lifts the cloth and I see a wonder: a loaf of freshly baked bread. It's all I can do not to exclaim out loud, "Wow!"

It feels like magic to see it there. Suddenly God is all around me and I'm eager to be fed. I can't wait for Jenny to tear into that bread. Suddenly there is grace and abundance upon abundance, like my life is full and I can have anything I want, even more. I already feel the crust on my tongue and the fluff of the bread filling my mouth. Yes, all this because of a loaf of bread. Understand how miraculous a drink of water can seem to one who is parched. Recognize how narrow a person's thinking can become when it seems what you want is impossible and scarcity is all you see. Know that I sat there lamenting my spiritual hunger and the absence of real bread. Then suddenly, there it is. All at once I feel the silliness of what I've been contemplating and the closeness of my Lord saying, "It's okay. You will be fulfilled in this and so much more."

As I deliver the chalice, though, I see others are perturbed by the chunks of bread in their hands. They're probably thinking, "Where are the wafers? They're so much easier." One person seems mortified when a piece breaks off and remains floating in the wine. A woman dips her bread but, in drawing it to her mouth, she drips wine on her hands. She shakes her head, embarrassed. I press my purificator onto her hand to absorb the wine and I smile. "It's okay," I whisper.

I can't say why—maybe because her frustration feels akin to what I've been turning over in my mind for months—but this is when I realize: what feeds me best won't always be simple and easy, like a pressed wafer. It will be messy and different. It will not be the same as it was months before because the Lord will have moved on to other things. I have to figure out how to follow. In this imperfection and brokenness I have to taste the Lord and trust.

One might say I've been manipulated, that the designed service has worked on me in a vulnerable state. I could have thought as much too if I had been sitting in a pew week after week and not engaged in all the activities that have made my worship life so messily busy the past few years. I may have grown cynical by now. I may have thought, "Oh, how clever! She preached about bread and there's the bread!" I could have been discomfited by the crumbs in the wine and thought them gross when I went to take my sip.

But I have been on a journey, even if only this one morning. And it has wearied me and broken me to the point where it is not a sense of cynicism that rises naturally from my heart—it is a sense of grace. This grace tells me that I matter despite the paltry, scattered nature of my thoughts. That I can have what I desire to sense God at work, even if it is simply a fluffy morsel of baked bread and not a pressed wafer. And think of this—how much more fulfilling will the pressed wafer be in the future because I had this moment?

And now I am grateful for all that has gone before on this morning—grateful for the doubt and hesitancy because it has brought me once again to this place of oneness with my God. Where would I be spiritually on this particular day if I had not come to church? Christ means for us to have life and to have it abundantly. Not to scrape in scarcity, to accept "less than," which had been my thinking only minutes before.

In time, perhaps as little as seven days, I will forget this lesson. And there will be more difficult Sunday mornings. But something within me, even on a cellular level, will remember this moment or the potential for such a moment. Some sort of assistance, maybe even the nudge of an angel whispering "get up and eat," will help me reach for it once more.

5

The Image Turns Back

LAUREN F. WINNER

A poem has changed my mind about the Eucharist. For the better part of two decades—since I was baptized in a Cambridge
college chapel, inaugurating my life not just as a Christian, but as
a Christian of the Anglican-Episcopal sort—I have been mildly
irked at my churches' habit of using those small round wafers during Communion. At the Methodist divinity school where I teach,
and at many of the Presbyterian or nondenominational churches
I've visited, the Lord's Supper usually features a loaf of bread,
sometimes baked by one of the communicants. But most of the
fifteen hundred or so Eucharists I've received, and all but two or

three of those I've celebrated, consecrate wafers. This has irritated me. I read John 6, and I long to celebrate the Eucharist with bread that more obviously evokes Jesus's words. If I want to understand that Jesus-in-the-Eucharist is real food, wouldn't the better ritual object be a baguette or a stottie, rather than a wafer that feels and tastes like Kleenex stiffened with glue? At church, we sing "Bread of Heaven, on thee we feed, for thou art our food indeed," and I find myself daydreaming about a parish bread guild; I imagine us baking ciabatta and Irish soda bread; I imagine Moravian love feasts.

Sometimes, I'm given a glimpse of how the wafer qua wafer might be instructive. Icons that depict manna in the wilderness as eucharistic wafers offer such a glimpse. They remind me that the whole point is that the host is not, in fact, ordinary bread, just as the manna was not ordinary bread—the host is precisely bread that is also the flesh of Jesus. The panary irregularity of the wafer guards against my mistaking the Eucharist for a meal that is made special because we remember, rather than eat, Jesus.

I'm wary of reducing a poem (or, for that matter, an icon or a sacrament) to its pedagogical potential—here's what it can teach us—but poems (and icons and sacraments) disclose, and when poems engage Christianity, they show us things about God and the Christian life that theological treatises cannot. It is a poem's disclosure that has latterly made me glad that the Eucharistic community in which I've landed prefers wafers to bread.

The most overtly eucharistic of Elizabeth Jennings's poems were published in the decade before her death in 2001, and, in my judgment, they're not her best poetry—they're a bit too direct. Yet they are right-headed: "the bread wraps / Christ thinly in it," she writes in "At Mass (I)"—"Time ceases when the gold ciborium's lid / Is lifted and Christ comes to us as still // As he was at his birth."[1] And, in "At Mass (II)," "The celebration works on us." When, after the Mass, we return to the ordinary world, we're able to see that

1. Jennings, *New Collected Poems*, 301–2.

world transfigured: "all the usual things // Are shining with right purpose."[2]

Those poems pose with economy—and, in the case of her word "thinly," with striking complexity—commonplace truths about the Eucharist. It is Jennings's "A Full Moon" that showed me something less commonplace, something I'd not yet seen:

> Tonight the full moon is the Host held up
> For everybody's eyes[3]

After those opening lines, Jennings limns biblical history ("we refused / To leave one Tree alone" but God's "overflowing grace / Gave us another chance") and diagnoses the human condition ("It seems we cannot bear for long / A simple goodness but must choose the wrong // Because it looks so sweet").[4] And then the poem returns to the lunar Eucharist:

> That Host-like moon shines where
> All can see him . . .
> That moon in silence can
> Elevate us till we long to know
> The Trinity's whole plan.[5]

The moon allows human beings to mimic the choreography of the Host: drawn heavenward by the full moon, we become Host-like, something "elevate[d]"—and, when we receive the moon as a Eucharist of sorts (when we see that the moon participates in the Eucharist), we are pulled by the moon past the moon to its Creator: "Nature was fashioned for this purpose. See / A moon remind us of God's ministry."[6]

On a straightforward reading, the poem means for me to look at the full moon and see the flesh of Christ. Jennings's evocation of the moon is not transcendentalism, not Emerson's learning "from

2. Jennings, *New Collected Poems*, 304–5.

3. Jennings, *New Collected Poems*, 314.

4. Jennings, *New Collected Poems*, 314.

5. Jennings, *New Collected Poems*, 314–15.

6. Jennings, *New Collected Poems*, 315.

nature the lesson of worship."[7] It is, rather, Jennings showing readers how to see the world as a Christian—how to see, as Christina Rossetti did, that "sparrow and lily . . . recall God's providence, seed His Word, earthly bread the Bread of Heaven, a plough the danger of drawing back"[8]; or how to see, as Justin Martyr did, the cross in ships' masts, unicorn horns, and human noses.

Jennings may not have anticipated that "The Full Moon" would help an American Episcopal priest appreciate her church's wafer—a loaf of artisanal ciabatta might make my Sunday Eucharist seem more like a real meal, but it wouldn't allow me to see the Eucharist in the sky at night. In "At Mass (II)," Jennings writes that "Every moment of enchantment we've / ever known . . . here is present."[9] Yes—and, like all the best metaphors, hers are recursive: showing the moon to be a Eucharist of sorts is enchantment that loops back around to enchant my wafer. The poem, like the Eucharist itself, has made an ordinary thing (a moon; a wafer) shine with its right purpose.

What Jennings has offered is not just a metaphor or simile: because the cosmos bears the image of its Creator, traces of Jesus really are there in the moon. Poetry is not first for didacticism, but teaching is one thing a poem can do, and I am grateful to have been instructed by Jennings's "Host-like moon." I like looking up at night and finding a vestige of Jesus; I prefer to live in a world that's enchanted, and not just commodified.

Ships' masts may partake of the cross and the moon a Eucharist, but only eyes trained to see the marks of the Maker in creation will notice. (Just as a piece of writing might carry the stylistic signature of Wallace Stevens or T. S. Eliot, but untrained readers won't perceive it.) Partakers of the Eucharist, too, need to be taught what to see. In the early church, bishops worried about the anticlimax of first Communion: "Perhaps you may say: I see something else; how do you tell me that I receive the Body of Christ?" wrote

7. Emerson, *Selected Essays*, 71.

8. Rossetti, *Letter and Spirit*, 131–32.

9. Jennings, *New Collected Poems*, 305.

Ambrose.[10] The newly baptized had to learn to see with "the eyes of the heart."

I have begun taking poetry lessons. I'd like to learn to write a poem. But I'd be satisfied if I could learn to see what's really there in the poems I read. (Maybe I'm being unfair to Jennings. Maybe her later Eucharistic poetry has formal excellences I don't know how to see.)

Yehuda Amichai's "I Studied Love" is another poem that joins the moon and liturgy. The narrator is a boy in synagogue, looking through the white lace partition that separates the sexes at prayer. He wishes to be with the women, wishes to pray the prayers that only women pray.

> And the faces of women like the face of the moon behind
>   the clouds
> or the full moon when the curtain parts: an enchanted
> cosmic order. At night we said the blessing
> over the moon outside, and I
> thought about the women.[11]

This, too, is instruction about figures and prayer. Amichai elongates the chain of associations that Jennings began—Jennings sees her liturgical artifact (the Eucharist) in a moon; Amichai first sees the moon in his liturgical artifact (the women's faces), and then he comes to find their faces in the moon.

The recursivity works like this: once you see that the moon is a Eucharist and your Eucharist a moon, then all that you know about one becomes a key for reading the other. You think about how the Eucharist is hidden, as the full moon is always really present, but often hidden. Remembering what your auntie taught you about herbs—that their healing properties are intensified if they're gathered under a plenilune—you sympathize with Christians in the Middle Ages, asking priests to celebrate the Eucharist in their gardens, knowing the Eucharistic crumbs would feed and magic their beets and lettuces. You ponder the long-held belief that the

---

10. Ambrose, *Myst.*, 9.50 (FOTC 44:23).

11. Amichai, *Open Closed Open*, 46.

full moon drives people crazy, and you think about the Eucharist as the "insanity of the cross."

"No poetic cliché is more weary than the moon,"[12] wrote one of Dickinson's biographers (before proceeding to hymn the art Dickinson made from that particular cliché). Perhaps the Eucharist is weary sometimes, too.

In one of those poems the Dickinson scholar loves, Dickinson likens the moon she sees through a window to a guillotined head. Of course, now that's what I think about as I sit beside the reserved sacrament on Good Friday.

As we sing, "O sacred head now wounded."

As we sing, "'Twas on that dark, that doleful night."

As we sing, "The moon, the stars, the universe, their maker's death bewail."

Bibliography

Ambrose. *Saint Ambrose: Theological and Dogmatic Works.* Fathers of the Church 44. Translated by Roy J. Deferrari. Washington, DC: Catholic University of America Press, 1963.

Amichai, Yehuda. *Open Closed Open.* Translated by Chana Bloch and Chana Kronfeld. New York: Harcourt, 2000.

Emerson, Ralph Waldo. *Ralph Waldo Emerson: Selected Essays.* Edited by Larzer Ziff. New York: Penguin, 1982.

Frank, Georgia. "'Taste and See': The Eucharist and the Eyes of Faith in the Fourth Century." *Church History* 70 (2001) 619–43.

Jennings, Elizabeth. *New Collected Poems.* Manchester: Carcanet, 2002.

Pickstock, Catherine. *After Writing: On the Liturgical Consummation of Philosophy.* Oxford: Wiley-Blackwell, 1997.

Rossetti, Christina. *Letter and Spirit: Notes on the Commandments.* London: SPCK, 1883.

Sewall, Richard B. *The Life of Emily Dickinson.* Cambridge: Harvard University Press, 1976.

12. Sewall, *Life of Emily Dickinson*, Vol. 1, 242.

6

The Play of the People

RODNEY CLAPP

As a child of four or five, I wanted a Superman costume for Christmas. Santa Claus obliged. I can still feel the keenness of my excitement. But quickly following it was a sense of loss and disappointment. I tore away the wrapping paper, opened the box, and shook free the shirt with its large red and yellow S—and there found a crushing message. On the hem was a warning that read, "Caution: This suit does not enable you to fly." In my child's imagination, I had anticipated donning the costume and leaping off Granddad's shed, then soaring above the treetops. That, of course, was not to be. But I still played dress-up, for hours at a time, garbed in my new present.

More than fifty-five years later, I keep playing dress-up. Now I dress up not as a Superman but, on many Sunday mornings, as a humble acolyte. I wear not a blue suit and a red cape, but a white alb and a colored scapular.

When my daughter became a teenager, she was invited to serve as an acolyte at our church. I thought it would be a wonderful thing to do with her. So, with her permission, I became an acolyte too—in my mid-forties.

My daughter has since grown up and left our church for her own pursuits, but I'm still an acolyte. In fact, it's hard to name a practice of church service I've enjoyed more. It brings me closer to the heart of the Eucharist, allows hands-on participation in the grand mysteries at the center of our faith. And in no way is that more true than in the privilege of being allowed to play with fire. As a wise priest told me, "All acolytes are pyromaniacs."

There are the candles, of course. But even more pleasing are the duties of the thurifer, the acolyte who bears the container (the thurible) of burning incense. I like to see billows of smoke wafting forth as the priest (and then the thurifer) swings the thurible. There should be an abundant smell and quite visible clouds drifting toward heaven, raising the ingathered prayers of the people. So I take pains to make red hot the coal that will set the incense fogging.

On one occasion, not long after our church had completed the building of a new wing, I went down to what we acolytes call the "fire room" to heat the coal and ready the thurible for censing. As I was transferring the heated coal to the thurible, the coal slipped from the tongs and fell to the cement floor. It shattered into several chunks.

I grabbed a broom to sweep up the glowing sparks and bits of charcoal, but failed to observe that the broom's bristles were nylon—and quickly the broom was ominously smoking from multiple spots. I rushed the broom into the adjacent kitchen and dunked it under running water. Then I returned to the fire room and ground out all the ashes with my foot until they were safe for sweeping. Everything was under control soon enough, but not before I imagined myself burning down the church, brand new wing and all.

The acolyte's life can be exciting. And in addition to the fire thing, there's bell-ringing, dressing in robed vestments like the clergy, and leading the parade of clergy and choir members into and out of the sanctuary.

Special occasions keep an acolyte on his or her toes. When the diocesan bishop visits, an acolyte designated the "bishop's chaplain" is assigned to assist the bishop throughout the liturgy. This is because the bishop has an ornate, peaked hat (the mitre), an equally ornate wood-and-silver shepherd's staff (the crozier), and, despite his or her exalted ecclesiastical office, only two hands.

The bishop's chaplain shadows the bishop throughout the liturgy, handing or taking from the bishop the mitre or the crozier as occasion dictates. I was reasonably relaxed before my first service as bishop's chaplain. Then someone who had performed those duties started telling me stories about embarrassing mistakes committed by bishop's chaplains of the past. One handed the mitre to the bishop backwards, so that when the august official rose and put on his hat, two ribbons hung down over his eyes. Another dropped the crozier, which not only clattered humiliatingly on the uncarpeted floor but also broke. The bishop had to carry it out of the service in two pieces.

In such ways acolytes get noticed. Ordinarily, though, acolytes are not noticed and are not supposed to be noticed. We are trained to be inconspicuous, like butlers or maids. As the *Shorter Oxford English Dictionary* defines it, the acolyte "performs subordinate duties."

All joshing aside, this is what I like most about being an acolyte. For me, at least, it's difficult not to be self-conscious while I'm worshiping. And that's particularly the case if I am preaching or otherwise "up front." What acolytes do is participate integrally in worship, yet all the while blend into the background of liturgy.

Clad in our simple albs, none of us makes (or fails to make) a fashion statement. We quietly carry vessels to and from the altar. We hold the book as the deacon reads the Gospel lesson. In these and other understated ways, we enable or facilitate eucharistic celebration and the prayer of the parish. An acolyte has done his or her job when the liturgy goes smoothly and, afterward, at Sunday lunch, no one in the congregation can remember exactly who served as acolytes that morning.

It is commonly said that liturgy is "the work of the people." This is because the Greek word *leitourgia* derives from the word for public (*lēitos*) and working (*ergos*). Now strictly speaking *leitourgia* was not the "work of the people" but "works performed for the people." In New Testament times, the word designated the building of bridges and aqueducts, structures for the common good and necessary to the conduct of everyday pursuits. Liturgy as work sustains the life of the community. Nevertheless, it is the case that this gift of liturgy, donated to the people, is something from which they benefit if they actively engage with it. In that sense there is indeed truth in the claim that liturgy invites "the work of the people."

All of this is true, and vital. But my reflections on acolyting point toward another aspect of the liturgy. With our dress-up, our ritual-following of prescribed gestures, our immersion in symbols, our rhythmic chanting, our synchronized movement, our lifting of voices in song, liturgy is the *play* of the people. In all these ways and more, liturgy resembles nothing so much as children's games.

Children play for no purpose. They simply have an abundance of energy and wonder, with which they engage one another and their world. They dance, skip rope, tussle with dogs, sing, build mud pies and dig holes, strut like their father or sashay like their mother, pretend in the garb of a parent or superhero, hide from and chase one another, bat and throw balls—all to no end and never as a means of production. If play produces anything, it is only more play. Children play to be, or, more precisely, simply as they be. They play without plans or rotas or to-do lists.

Likewise, if we see the liturgy in its depths, we will know that it has no purpose. As the Roman Catholic theologian Romano Guardini states, "The liturgy has no purpose or, at least, it cannot be considered from the standpoint of purpose. It is not a means which is adapted to attain a certain end—it is an end in itself."[1] We can undertake nothing more important, and at the same time nothing more playful, than liturgy. Liturgy is the worship of God, not any production of humanity. True, worship may eventuate in human goods—peace, joy, the cultivation of character—but these are by-products, not the aim of worship.

Guardini looks to two scriptural texts for his biblical undergirding of worship as play. First, he cites Ezekiel's vision of the flaming cherubim, who "every one of them went straight forward, whither the impulse of the Spirit was to go . . . and they turned not when they went . . . ran and returned like flashes of lightning . . . went . . . and stood . . . and were lifted up from the earth . . ." (1:4, 12, 17, 20). Here the virtuosi of worship, with no other end or skill except to worship, are gamboling lightning, angels raised from dull earth by their innate levity. Comments Guardini: "They are only pure motion, powerful and splendid, acting according to the direction of the Spirit, desiring nothing save to express [their] inner drift and . . . interior glow and force. They are the living image of the liturgy."[2]

Second, Guardini recalls Proverbs 8:30–31: "I was with him, forming all things, and was delighted every day, playing before him at all times, playing in the world . . . ." Wisdom, the pre-incarnate Logos, dances and rejoices in sheer creation and creation's sustenance and diversity. The "Son plays before the Father," and what higher endorsement might we need for us to do the same?[3]

We should not instrumentalize worship, and yet I am struck by how radical are the effects of claiming and recognizing liturgy as play. Little if anything can reinforce more how creation and redemption depend on God. Humanity cannot create or save itself.

1. Kuehn, ed., *The Essential Guardini*, 148.

2. Kuehn, *The Essential Guardini*, 148–49.

3. Kuehn, *The Essential Guardini*, 149.

We are created and saved by God alone. And God's creative and redemptive acts are first and final. God acts in prevenient and salvific grace. We are called but to respond, and even then only in the power of the Spirit. Quite apart from any human initiative, God the Father has acted in the Son through the Spirit to make and to restore creation. Worship is but celebratory play of this first and final act beyond all acts. Participating in it, we are reminded who and what we are—creatures, wonderfully made and yet more wonderfully restored.

Integral to corporate worship, and flowing out of it into all other worship, is the attitude and practice of contemplative prayer. The contemplative witnesses to the truth that God has acted and will act apocalyptically, and nothing more—certainly nothing greater—need be said or done. The contemplative calls us to recognize that we are permitted to do nothing, and yet God has done everything. To contemplate produces or constructs nothing: it simply lets be, and soaks in what preeminently is. Contemplation's cash value is zero, so it may be the only practice left that can escape the inundation of neoliberalism and unrestrained capitalism's commodifying reduction of our lives. Perhaps Guardini had something like this in mind when he said, "Truth is a power, provided you don't demand an immediate effect, but rather have patience and expect that it will take a long time [before you see results]. . . . If anywhere, then here, lack of purpose is the greatest power."[4]

In all events, we can note Guardini's summary of liturgy as the play of the people.

> The soul must learn to abandon, at least in prayer, the restlessness of purposeful activity; it must learn to waste time for the sake of God, and to be prepared for the sacred game with sayings and thoughts and gestures, without always immediately asking "why?" and "wherefore?" It must learn not to be continually yearning to do something, to attack something, to accomplish something

4. Kuehn, *The Essential Guardini*, 8.

useful, but to play the divinely ordered game of liturgy in liberty and beauty and holy joy before God.[5]

This is what I have learned through acolyting and forty years of other liturgical worship. In worship, in holy play, we engage in a game with one another and most of all with God. There is no end or purpose to it. It is a glorious waste of time. We come to worship with no duty or responsibility to get something done, no task to accomplish, no to-do list to trudge through. We come to dress up and to play and revel in the playing. And in liturgy, we may truly be able to fly.

Bibliography

Kuehn, Heinz R., ed. *The Essential Guardini,* Chicago: Liturgy Training, 1997.

5. Kuehn, *The Essential Guardini,* 152.

7

Bad Episcopalian

Melissa Deckman Fallon

I'm a bad Episcopalian. At least, I feel that way when it comes to worship.

When I say bad Episcopalian, I am channeling Roxane Gay, who declares that she's a bad feminist in her book of the same title. For years, Gay says, she shunned the word feminist because she felt that feminism involved impossible standards to uphold. How could she like pink, read fashion magazines, and listen to rap music and still consider herself a feminist? Yet she has come to see that while she is a flawed human who makes mistakes, she also knows that the basic goals of feminism, in its belief that men and women ought to be afforded equal opportunities, offer her guiding principles for how she writes, reads, and lives. She writes in *Bad Feminist*, "I do stray from these principles, but I also know it's okay when I do not live up to my best feminist self."[1]

I would never shun the word Episcopalian to describe myself, but much like Gay, I worry about being a bad Episcopalian. In my mind a good Episcopalian is one who attends church weekly, serves on the altar guild, and leads a Bible study in her home. I do not live up to that definition. Far from it. Attendance at worship for me is not nearly as regular as it should be. As I work full-time as a college professor, juggling other community duties with being a mom and wife for a family I adore, sometimes the appeal of brunch, grocery shopping, paper grading, or weeding the yard comes first on a Sunday morning. (Weeding is not appealing, but sometimes necessary!) Life often has a way of interfering with worship. Or more precisely, I let other aspects of my life interfere.

The shame of this situation is that I derive solace and enjoyment from the Episcopal worship service. It wasn't always that way. I am Episcopalian by choice, having been raised in a different Christian denomination. When I married my husband, who was raised Roman Catholic, we looked for a faith tradition that worked for both of us. The Episcopal Church's social justice mission and ordination of women spoke to me. The faith tradition in which I was raised was more conservative theologically, but I chose to be confirmed as an Episcopalian because the Nicene Creed affirmed for me the essentials of my own Christian beliefs—belief in the Holy Trinity, the resurrection, and the hope that eternal salvation brings.

But the worship service—whose liturgy was very familiar to my husband, a former Catholic altar boy—was, in a word, *different* from what I was used to. Why the formality and fancy dress for worship leaders? Why do parishioners have to respond in unison with canned, rehearsed phrases? Why does the sermon come in the middle of the service—shouldn't that be the finale? Why can't Episcopalians sing some newer, catchier songs, in keys that are

1. Gay, *Bad Feminist*, xiii.

within my range? And why on earth do Episcopalians insist on singing every verse?!

However, over time, I got used to the rhythm of the liturgy. While the scripted call and response found in the Book of Common Prayer was decidedly not a part of the worship services of my own upbringing—I'd say my childhood services were far more laid-back, the songs were more modern, and the star of the show was certainly the pastor—I grew to like hearing my voice be one among many in unison, to be part of a service in which there is value to having *all* members play a part. And unlike the services of my youth, Episcopal worship is far from passive. It is engaging and physical: a workout for body, mind, and spirit. While I'm dubious about whether Sunday morning service burns as many calories as my typical run, experiencing the physical components, whether kneeling for prayer, moving forward to receive communion, or extending my hand to a fellow parishioner for the peace, have all become enjoyable parts of the service for me.

However, my favorite parts of the service are the quieter ones, particularly prayer. I pray a lot during the day by myself and, at dinner, our family says grace together. Prayer has always been a source of comfort. And I'm not alone—data from the Pew Research Center finds that a majority of Americans report praying every day. Social science abounds with studies showing its positive effects. But there is something powerful about praying in God's house, whether I recite the Lord's Prayer in unison with the rest of the congregation, or, after communion, as parishioners wave greetings to the people returning to their pews or smaller children fidget in their seats, I close my eyes and pray silently to God. I find great meaning in the fact that millions of other Episcopalians and Anglicans worldwide are reciting the same words from the Book of Common Prayer or quietly ad libbing direct prayers to God in their own way. I like to think that there is strength in numbers when it comes to both forms of prayer in worship.

In our modern world, Americans are increasingly atomized, isolated from our neighbors and one another. Rather than be part of a physical community with actual human beings, Americans seem increasingly content to log onto their devices to escape into their social media worlds, as the pull of their posts or Instagram photos being liked, re-tweeted, or shared holds great, addictive appeal. Yet social science research shows that the effects of such isolation are profound and disturbing. As a result, I worry about trends showing that the numbers of Americans who worship regularly in communal fashion are decreasing dramatically, particularly among Millennials. This makes participating in the long-held rituals of The Episcopal Church all the more meaningful—a nourishing antidote to modern life in which Americans retreat into the comforts of home or the silos of digital echo chambers. I hope to model to my two sons the importance not just of belief in God, or in the wonder-working power of Jesus (as the old hymn attests), but also being part of a faith community. Belief is essential, certainly, but showing up is part of the process, too.

Diana Butler Bass writes in her beautiful book *Grounded* that the organized, "vertical" religion that marks much of Western Christian theology, in which people experience God through religious services or sacraments that "act as a holy elevator between God above and those muddling around below in the world,"[2] is not meeting the religious needs of an increasing number of individuals. Instead, she argues that Americans, who are still a nation of religious seekers, are experiencing God in more direct ways, connecting with nature, their neighbors, and even the stars, realizing that the church is not the only sacred space. I don't necessarily disagree with Bass's conclusions—there are certainly moments when I see God in a beautiful sunset as my husband and I walk our dog or in the laughing eyes of a child. But for me, worship in God's house still has the power to inspire and complete me.

I may not be a good Episcopalian yet, but I'm working on it. Every service attended, whether it's weekly or less than weekly, allows me to engage in the practice of becoming a better Episcopalian. Sometimes my family can only manage a brief, thirty-minute service on Sunday evenings that features simple music, some scripture, and a brief message from the priest. It's a terrific way to

2. Bass, *Grounded*, 12.

close out our weekend and to be ready to face the week ahead. But as I get older, I am increasingly grateful for the knowledge that our God is a forgiving God who loves despite our many faults. God's message of grace and forgiveness is available to all—no matter how many times I attend church (or decide to go to brunch with my family instead), which is something I learned in worship.

Bibliography

Bass, Diana Butler. *Grounded: Finding God in the World—A Spiritual Revolution.* San Francisco: HarperOne, 2015.

Gay, Roxane. *Bad Feminist: Essays.* New York: Harper Perennial, 2014.

8

Singing in the Choir
on Sunday Morning

STEPHEN FOWL

It's Sunday morning, and I am back in my seat feeling an odd combination of gratitude for Christ's body and blood shed for me, and the residual taste of the consecrated wine. I clear my throat and join the choir as we lead the congregation through our communion hymns. The choir always receives first and then we return to our seats on either side of the central aisle of the cathedral. Everyone else passes between the two sides of the choir on their way to the altar. I know I will marvel at the way our organist and choirmaster, Ken Brown, provides seamless transitions between such hymns as "What Wondrous Love Is This?" and the rousing

"We Are Marching in the Light of God." The singing here is usually straightforward, and the bass line is often relatively simple. This gives me the freedom to watch everyone as the line of people slowly moves to the communion rail.

There are familiar faces I have worshipped with for many decades. We raised our children together and we are now contemplating the empty nest as well as thinking about how we will care for aging parents. I see people who were my age when we started worshipping at the cathedral. They are a bit more stooped, slower moving. Our ushers help them get up the three stairs to the altar or someone will serve them in their seat. If the demands of singing still allow me to watch closely, I am likely to see someone I have not seen in a while or a new person I don't know. Perhaps I can offer a prayer for someone I know has been struggling. Other times, I am simply filled with gratitude for their presence. We have a large number of immigrants, asylees, and refugees from West Africa. The gorgeous bright colors of their Sunday outfits always make me smile. Because we have a soft space for young children at the back of the church, those families bring up the rear. The parents will have one child in their arms while they guide or pull or push an older child. I am amazed that a church that did not seem very full when I processed in now has a communion line stretching the length of the aisle.

For nearly thirty years I have been a member of the choir at the Cathedral of the Incarnation in Baltimore. We are a pretty good choir, especially when one considers that, with just a few exceptions, we are volunteers. Many cathedral choirs are composed of professional or semi-professional singers. Their sound and musicianship are far better than ours. I recognize that professional choirs offer a genuine service to the worshipping community. On the other hand, as a group of volunteers, we have the advantage of being part of the community. Nevertheless, some Sundays I wish we were a better choir, more rigorous in our preparation, more selective in whom we let in, more demanding in the type of music we sing. On those days my worship is pretty truncated, frustrated, and whiney.

More often I am simply filled with gratitude for the people I sing with. They, like me, sing because they want to offer their song to God in aid of the whole congregation's worship. My gratitude to God for my fellow choir members is rarely dependent on how we sing on any given Sunday. It arises from the fact that I know the people behind the voices. I know what their day-to-day lives are like; I know what being in the choir means to them and what we mean to each other. I see in flesh and bone that God calls all sorts and conditions of people into the kingdom, people whom I would never have encountered otherwise. They and I come with trials and sorrows and joys and we offer a song to God.

What happens on Sunday is always an adventure in grace. Sometimes the music shines even when rehearsal has not gone well. Sometimes we bungle a piece nailed in rehearsal. Sometimes we are in over our heads and we simply survive to sing another day. God takes what we offer and uses it to touch someone. Of course, many times the hard work of rehearsal combines with hearts tuned to the Spirit and the result is a glorious offering to God. Even such successes, however, are the working out of grace. It is important to remember this, particularly when things go well. It is too easy to think that the success of our worship depends on the choir, or the preacher, or the celebrant when it really depends on God's unrelenting and eager openness to our offerings. Remember, this is the God to whom all hearts are open, all desires known, and from whom no secrets are hid.

Being in the choir is not simply about singing. It is also Christian formation. You enter as a volunteer, but are also quickly invited to take on a set of obligations. It's not just rehearsal on Thursday and church on Sunday. In dozens of ways, large and small, we take care of each other—support for the new mom, a shower for an expectant choir couple, meals for those bereaved or in other difficulties, prayers for all occasions.

You also learn quickly that we each have our foibles, our distinct mannerisms, and pet peeves, especially when it comes to church music. Most of the time we handle these with the right combination of teasing and grace. Sometimes we get it wrong, however, and that can be painful. When you sing you make your-self vulnerable. Blunders and mistakes are part of singing. At our best, we can laugh at these and move on. It can be painful when you're convinced you are singing well, or at least well enough, and someone has to tell you that you are not. More than a few choir relationships have been damaged by criticism that came at the wrong time, from the wrong person, in the wrong way. At our best, we take our singing seriously, but we don't take ourselves too seriously. Even that attitude, however, is a gift of grace.

I've spent more than half my life singing in this choir. It has taught me something about how Christians grow old. I know a time is coming when I will not be able to continue in the choir. I know this because I see others who have been my choir comrades now sitting in the pews unable to do what they once enjoyed as much as I do. Age and infirmity eventually undermine our capaci-ties to sing. At such a time I will need to learn how to inhabit a new space in the body. I have some concerns here. There is a common saying, often erroneously attributed to Augustine, that the one who sings prays twice. Regardless of who said it, I think I agree. The act of singing to God and the words sung are both forms of prayer. Indeed, sometimes singing helps me pray words I would find strange or even objectionable to speak in prayer. I worry that once I can no longer sing or sing well enough to remain in the choir, I will lose some of my already limited capacities for prayer. If, as Paul notes, singing is one of the ways in which we allow the word of Christ to dwell in us richly, how can I still let the word of Christ dwell in me? God willing, I have some years to figure this out. I hope to learn from my retired comrades how they have made this transition so that when the time comes and I can no longer sing as I do now, I can still pray and the word of Christ can still find a place to dwell in me.

Of course, even if one does not sing in a choir, singing may be an essential aspect of liturgy. From the earliest days of the church singing was deeply woven into the fabric of Christian worship. Both Ephesians 5:19 and Colossians 3:16 encourage believers to sing. In Ephesians Paul says, "be filled with the Spirit addressing each other in psalms and hymns and spiritual songs, singing and making melody in your hearts to the Lord."[1] Singing is tied to being filled with the Spirit. In addition, singing has a dual focus. It is directed to God and to "each other." I presume that this means that the Spirit uses our singing as both a way of praising and worshipping God and as a way of encouraging our brothers and sisters to do likewise.

This idea is picked up in Colossians where Paul writes, "Let the word of Christ dwell in you richly; teach and admonish one another in all wisdom and with gratitude in your hearts sing psalms and hymns and spiritual songs to God." Again singing has the dual function of helping us to address both God and each other. Moreover, singing lets the word of Christ dwell in us. Finally, Paul assumes that by singing we give concrete testimony to our heartfelt gratitude to God. God is both object and subject of the praises Christians sing. We are a singing people.

During the distribution of the bread and the wine, when almost everyone has received, the organist begins to play the final communion hymn. We use the same piece throughout a whole liturgical season. In Epiphany we may sing "I Want to Walk as a Child of the Light." In Ordinary time, we usually sing the Taize chorus "Jubilate Deo" as a round. When the last person has been served, we all stand and continue our hymn, singing to God and singing to each other. We receive God's gifts through our mouths and we offer gifts back to God with our mouths. This carries us into the post-communion prayer when we thank God for joining us together with Christ and each other, reminding us that though we are many and diverse, we are one body because we have just shared one bread and one cup.

---

1. Translations are the author's.

9

The Great Celestial-Terrestrial Choir

Amy E. Richter

It's probably a bad thing in a priest, but sometimes I find it easier to believe in demons than angels. This is one of the reasons I need to be in church every Sunday: demons are on the loose and I would rather spend time with angels.

I want to relegate demons to Bible Land, a faraway country having no borders contiguous with my own, a realm where other improbable creatures exist as well, like snakes that advise on dietary restrictions and angels who provide travel directions in dreams. While some parts of Jesus's story translate easily to my own terrain,

I want other parts to stay strange or quaint, dismissible because I know better than they can in that place untouched by modern science and medicine. Where I live, we don't need exorcists; we have pharmaceuticals.

Perhaps demons are like talking snakes and other things we dismiss as not belonging here because we're afraid of them. The descriptions of the demon-possessed in the Gospels are frightening: unseen malevolent spirits hijack their bodies, pilfer the contents, gut interiors, and vandalize exteriors. The possessed are doomed for demolition unless Jesus comes to the rescue and does what no one else had authority to do: command them to vacate the premises. On one occasion, he evicts demons identifying themselves as "Legion" (the name of a Roman military unit of hundreds of men; are demons braggarts as well as squatters?) into a herd of swine, angering the pig farmers, scaring the stuffing out of the townspeople, and adding to my list of stories to tell young confirmands when they say the Bible is boring.

But Jesus evidently believed in demons, so maybe I should too. Besides, I've seen them. Okay, not them directly, but their carnage, or something that comes close to the Gospel descriptions that may very well be better described as chemical imbalance, misfiring neurons, or genetic mutation. Yet right before my eyes I see people turned to husks, empty except for something inside that wants to control them for a purpose counter to their own wellbeing and wholeness. I've seen parents, siblings, and spouses beside themselves with grief and frustration, wondering what happened to the child, the brother, the sister, the partner they once knew, seemingly replaced by someone unrecognizable, unreachable, untamable. I have heard them wail their own words of despair, "Nothing makes this better!"

Perhaps that's the hardest part of the story to fathom: Jesus's ability to terminate the possession, to return to a parent someone they recognize with a command. In my country of diagnoses, prescriptions, and therapies, there can be help and hope, but the progress is more halting, vaults forwards, jerks into reverse, and sometimes stalls or never comes.

So yes, I believe there are forces at work that seek to rip us apart, shred us, leave us empty and unrecognizable, in part by destroying our capacity for relationship, and maybe illness is one of the weapons they use against us. In the Bible, they're called demons, and Jesus believes in them. Maybe my believing in them, at least in a sense, makes me just a little like Jesus.

But Jesus also believed in angels, so maybe I should take them seriously too.

Here again, I've been quick to translate angels away from my world. I'm not alone. The word also means "messenger," so anyone who brings a welcome message can be an angel, right? Especially if they show up unexpected, at just the right time, maybe even with the quintessential angelic opening line, "Fear not."

Like the time my tire blew out on a busy highway. I managed to steer onto the grassy median and wished I had brought my charger so my dead cell phone could be the lifeline it's supposed to be. I wished it hadn't been decades since my father showed me how to change a tire and that I could remember what he had said about where absolutely never to put the jack. Three heavily tattooed, buzz-cut, muscled young men in a giant pickup truck, tailgate covered in pro-gun bumper stickers, pulled up in front of my ancient tan Toyota Camry and said, "Don't worry, Ma'am. Let's get your spare."

I was on my way quickly, grateful for their assistance. When I explained my tardiness at my destination, the response was, "God sent you angels." Maybe. They did swoop in, unexpected, and scare me speechless. They reassured me, probably in response to the look on my face, "Don't worry." (Fear not, Ma'am, actually. I appreciated the polite address, even though it makes me feel a little old, and surely angels are older than I?) And they did get me out of a bind. Who knows? Maybe they saved my life. I did go on my way rejoicing, but they looked pretty human to me. Do we have to promote humans who behave kindly to angelic rank?

I also bristle at new agey treatments of angels, at least those I've seen that turn angels into beings I can manipulate into making my dreams for prosperity come true if I know the right invocations.

I believe that the Divine wants to give me a life of abundant joy, but that joy might come in spite of my desires, not because of them, and the abundance unleashed on folks visited by angels in the Bible often has them experiencing things like unplanned pregnancies and becoming refugees. The Bible has made me suspicious of angels who promise they will deliver my version of my best self.

But there they are, honest-to-God angels in church every Sunday. Right where and when I need them: *with Archangels and all the company of heaven* as we join our voices with theirs as we *sing this hymn to proclaim the glory of your Name: Holy, Holy, Holy Lord, God of power and might, heaven and earth are full of your glory.* They carry on singing, apparently "for ever," while what's future for us punctures our present and for one magnificent moment we are all a part of a unified terrestrial-celestial choir.

This makes me happy. I look at the congregation, which this morning includes a woman whose increasing dishevelment and the rambling messages she's left on my voicemail lead me to believe a disease of the brain is wrapping her in its clutches. There's a man who last week, when I was greeting at the door after the service, pressed a small metal disc into my palm of what he called "the most precious metal on earth," though I recognize it as a congealed mass of cigarette packaging foil. I know where he lives; it may be the most precious item he has to offer, a genuine sacrifice. Demons lurk close by and our community needs to do what we can to love and care for these vulnerable people. I also see the woman who has been a messenger of glad tidings in our community, bringing the good news of Jesus to the children to whom she gives safe harbor during the long unstructured days of summer, and the man whose message to the young people he tutors is that they can learn and there is help and love and care all around them, embodied love and not just a wish.

In that moment, every Sunday, we sing together with ranks of angels and the whole company of heaven to the God whose power and might isn't far off, but here; and isn't contained here but fills all things and all time, including the time when we won't need diagnoses and medicines and kind humans won't seem so exceptional to the norm that we label them angels. In just a few minutes after our song, we will take into our hands *the body of Christ, the bread of heaven*, which is both ethereal and real. I can feel it and taste it and smell it and see it, enough senses to cover any that are failing. If the bread-body is real, maybe the celestial sections of our Sanctus-singing chorus are too.

I'm counting on it. I even I feel it some Sundays, although it feels more like a fullness in my heart than feathers brushing my face. I know that the whole company of heaven is singing with my congregation, and that the company includes people I love and will be reunited with some day, and then for longer than for a moment on Sunday mornings.

I know, I know, I'm trying hard to be a scholar of the Bible, and the whole timing of how the final time will unfold is up for debate, and are the dead already enjoying heaven or will we all have to wait until some big round up at the end time, and what is time to the dead, anyway? It's still a mystery. But we sing or say our way into this mystery every Sunday when we join our voices with theirs and sing praise to the God in whom we all live and move and have our being, who holds us and loves us all.

And during the Sanctus, while I may not actually be apprehending the vibrations of my mother's voice with the mechanics of my inner ear, I can hear her. It's not just the memory of standing next to her in church as she moved her finger along the lines of music in the hymnal so my little child self soaked in how a line of music works as well as the phonics of churchy phrases like, *Just as I am, without one plea; Lift high the cross, the love of Christ proclaim*; and *Abide with me*. It's not just remembering her strong soprano voice keeping the tempo she thought the hymn should be played at, trying to sing the organist in our little church into picking it up a notch. The memories are vivid and aided by this Sanctus-singing, but my Sunday experience is of presence as well as nostalgia.

This part of the liturgy has become more and more important to me as I know more and more beloved ones, faithful people, for whom *life is changed not ended*, as we say in the preface for the eucharistic prayer at funerals. Here is the promise: *When our mortal body lies in death, there is prepared for us a dwelling place eternal in the heavens.* Apparently, the space between that dwelling place and our earthly altars gets pierced on a regular basis. I get to hear my mom sing again.

Does she hear me too?

Sometimes people ask whether their beloved departed ones are able to visit them or direct them or offer guidance or protection. Sometimes someone asks the question and I think the asking is a way to see if it's safe to tell me they think they do. "Do the dead turn into angels?" someone else asks. I don't think so. Especially since there's no evidence of that in the Bible, and, besides, humans are already made in the image of God (Genesis 1) or only a little lower than angels, or even God (Psalm 8), depending on who is doing the translating, so why bother becoming an angel when you can stay human? Jesus was fully human; why would we want to be something different from him?

Sometimes I think the question results from the feeling of absence, that real, genuine absence, the hole in our heart when someone who used to be readily accessible by phone or email or text or in person, isn't any longer. Are they entirely accessible now? If so, I could really use some guidance!

I was blessed in my parents. I know they enjoyed being parents. Taking care of me and my siblings gave them pleasure amidst the aggravations, headaches, frustrations, and fears that were also part of the deal in raising me to adulthood and accompanying me on that journey until their deaths. They were caring people whose personal and professional lives in social work and church work meant their days were filled with giving guidance, love, direction, encouragement, advice, correction, and reassurance to the people in their charge. There's a lot I don't know about it yet, but I'm pretty sure heaven is supposed to be my parents' heaven too, not just a place from which they have a better vantage point on my life now than when we depended on wifi or cellphone coverage. If heaven is a place where they can get some rest, rather than worrying about me, as I know they used to, maybe part of my spiritual maturation is letting them get that rest for a change. Maybe heaven should be a place of rejoicing, rest, and the nearer presence of God, not a peephole through which they continue to try their best to raise me.

So when I think about wanting my parents, which I still do, maybe it's enough to meet in church on Sundays. After all, they were the ones who taught me to show up here every week. They were the ones who taught me to stick it out even when the organist plays a dancing hymn like a dirge. They taught me worship is a place where I'm going to meet and practice compassion for people who suffer and fight against all kinds of conditions not of their own making, suffering that makes them fearful to others, diseases that make other people want to banish them rather than pray and give for their healing, or study and strive for cures and treatments. They taught me that not only will Jesus show up in word and sacrament, tangible as the host in my hand, but I will get to sing with genuine angels and all the company of heaven.

10

Let Light Perpetual Shine
upon Them

CAMERON DEZEN HAMMON

I was confirmed an Episcopalian by the bishop of Texas shortly before my father died. He'd been ill a long time, most of my life, and when he was dying I sometimes tried to talk to him about God. Our conversations went like this:

"Jesus loves you," I'd say.

"What for?"

"He just . . . does."

"Does Jesus know you're Jewish?" He'd erupt into laughter.

My father was Jewish, and in his mind, so was I. My mother isn't Jewish, and when I was growing up in New Jersey I was considered a gentile by my Jewish friends and neighbors. But my identity was clear to my father. He was Jewish. I was Jewish. End of story. But it wasn't so clear to me.

I wanted to be Jewish, but in truth my father's Judaism was mostly rumor, and thus, so was mine. His was a non-observant Russian family who came to America around the turn of the last century, most likely to escape the violent pogroms that resulted in the deaths of thousands of Jews and sparked the exodus out of Europe of millions more. My father never talked about his family, but the Judaism he inherited from them imparted a sense of identity to him, and comfort. It was a source of pride, but it was not something with which he engaged on a day-to-day basis. Maybe it was a memory of familial trauma, or maybe it just didn't suit him. Whatever his reasons, my father never studied Hebrew, and never belonged to a synagogue. He was not Bar Mitvah'd as a young boy, and I was not Bat Mitvah'd as a girl. He ate bacon, and shellfish, and I never saw him wear a yarmulke. But we celebrated Rosh Hashanah and Yom Kippur and sometimes even Sukkot with my parents' Jewish friends. We always had a menorah during Hanukah. I went to dozens of Shabbat dinners and learned many of the blessings by heart. I was studying music, so I learned the mysterious words and melodies of the prayers the same way I learned songs for my recitals—by ear. To this day I can recite the blessing of the candles from memory. "*Baruch ata Adonai, Eloheinu Melech ha-olam, asher kidshanu b'mitzvotav vitzivanu l'hadlik ner shel Shabbat.*" In English: "Blessed are you, Lord our God, King of the Universe, who sanctified us with the commandment of lighting the Shabbat candles." This liturgy was a comfort to me. But as a child I didn't understand the prayer. Why *King*? What does *sanctify* mean? I also failed to understand my father's refusal to practice his religion with any sort of commitment. Formal membership had no bearing on the way he saw his religious identity.

I wanted to belong to something. I wanted somewhere to go every Friday night and Saturday morning, or even Sunday morning, not just at the odd invitation of a friend, but as a part of the rhythm of my life. After my parents divorced I left my Jewish aspirations behind and fell into a whirlwind romance with a version of evangelicalism I found through a small house church that called itself "Tribe." It had been started by a handful of young, British expats who moonlit as artists and DJs. It was the late 90s in New York City. There were church services in bars, there was gender equality, and social justice, and coffee, and cool music. Theirs was a kind of small-batch evangelicalism, without the political markings of what came later, of a kind I'd never seen before and haven't seen since. I was baptized on the beach at Coney Island. I'd finally found my community. When I told my father about my conversion he asked, "Do these people know you're Jewish?"

I went on to spend fourteen years as an evangelical. I found a path into full-time ministry as a music minister, a "worship leader" in the native parlance. I moved from New York to Texas, and pretty soon the Christianity I practiced went from small batch to quasi-Southern Baptist. It wasn't a good fit for me. I'd never ascribed to the conservative political beliefs many I met in evangelical churches held—I'd always considered myself socially progressive. But during those years, years I now think of as a wilderness, I kept my views to myself. I'm not proud of my silence during that time. I wish I'd had the courage to speak up. Instead, I tried to look the other way when my beliefs conflicted with my friends' and colleagues' beliefs. But eventually, right around the time the 2016 election was ramping up, I could no longer look the other way. I hit a wave of spiritual doubt not only in the tenets of Christian belief, but in the way Christianity is practiced in America. The community I'd long been a part of seemed to drift further and further into rhetorical madness in its efforts to elect a B-list celebrity to the office of president. I couldn't think of myself as an evangelical anymore, but what could I think of myself as? I didn't know.

That was when I found The Episcopal Church, or rather, it found me.

I was invited to sing at a Palm Sunday service at St. Mark's, a congregation on Houston's south side, not far from where I live with my husband and daughter. The church itself was unlike any other I'd previously sung in. It was old and pretty. There was stained glass. There were liturgical songs, with mysterious lyrics and melodies. I struggled to learn them. They were so different from the three-chord folk-rock songs I'd been playing in churches for years. "Still want to be an Episcopalian?" my husband asked winkingly, when I was slowly plunking out the Gloria on our piano for the thirteenth time. I shrugged. I didn't know what I wanted to be, but I knew I could learn the liturgical songs. I knew I could commit them to memory.

When my father was in the final stages of his battle with cancer, his doctor recommended he move into a rehabilitation facility—it was really a nursing home with a nicer sounding name. His children, me among them, agreed. It wasn't safe for him to continue living on his own, and it had become clear that he needed around-the-clock care—something we couldn't provide for him—our homes were too small, our lives too complicated. He'd fallen more than once. He was having a hard time preparing his meals, taking his medicine. He wasn't happy about the doctor's recommendation, but he went. He argued with his caregivers at the nursing home. He argued with his children. He argued with his doctor, and then the nursing home's director, a woman named Carol. He told Carol, during one of their arguments, more than he'd told me about his sense of Jewish identity. He wanted his body to be cared for by a Jewish funeral home when the time came. He wanted his body to be put in the care of people who shared his faith, people who knew what to do, knew how to follow the proper protocols.

"We'll have to act quickly," Carol told me when she called, before sunrise, to tell me he was gone. "It's a Jewish holiday," she explained. My father died on Sukkot, so it was a race against time to contact the Jewish funeral home in his town and make sure they transported his remains before the festivities would commence, and Jewish businesses would close. I trusted Carol, and then I trusted the Jewish funeral home to honor his wishes. And they did.

I was confirmed a few years after that first Palm Sunday service. I eventually wrote a new melody for the Gloria, and we sing it every week during the service I now lead music for at St. Mark's. I often think that my participation in The Episcopal Church has allowed me to continue calling myself a Christian. It's allowed me to stay connected to faith in a way that also makes room for my grief—not just about my father's death, but about the death of the idealistic evangelicalism I fell in love with so many years ago. I still field questions from people I used to worship with: Do you still believe? Are you praying? How can you believe in [insert progressive social issue] and still call yourself a Christian? My evangelical friends want to make sure I still belong. Maybe they wonder if they themselves belong. I never belonged, not really. I think of the way my father regarded his Jewish identity, until the very end of his life. Is that confidence of belonging available to those of us who identify as Christians? Even when our memberships lapse, our views waver, or our alignments shift or change? If I were to pray, I would pray for this: that we are able to offer each other, and ourselves, that kind of grace.

I was supposed to lead a 5 p.m. Rite II service the day my father died, and though the priest assured me I could take the night off, I went to St. Mark's anyway. I couldn't sing, my throat was swollen from crying. But I wanted to hear my father's name called during the Prayers of the People—"Give to the departed eternal rest." I wanted to hear his Jewish name called out in the warm, wooden church, the lights low, the last daylight cutting through the stained glass.

It isn't the sense of progressivism that keeps me Episcopalian, though that's important to me. It's the liturgy. I allow myself to enter and re-enter the story of God through the mysterious words and melodies, and I always have. Even when, especially when, my belief wanes, or falters, or finds no purchase, as it often does. I don't know what I believe about eternity, but I hope there is rest there, like the prayer suggests. "Let light perpetual shine upon them." I gripped the pew in front of me as my father's name was called, and I was reminded of all those high holidays we spent with friends, the Bat Mitzvahs, the sense of community, the faith of those around me. "We praise you for your saints who have entered into joy." I hope to have the sort of faith my father had. I hope, when it's my time, that the practices and prayers will provide a proper send-off for me. "May we also come to share in your heavenly kingdom." I hope that there will be a community to gather around my loved ones, a pew for my own daughter to grip. It wasn't my faith that got me through that night and many nights since. It was the congregation's faith that carried me, still carries me. Their faith. And their voices.

11

Spreading Blessing to Those Who Don't Work for It

Liturgical Reflections from a Cross-Cultural Missionary

DUANE ALEXANDER MILLER

It is Sunday in Madrid. I wear my cassock and surplice and sweat in the *calid* Spanish summer. Many locals have left the city for the coast or the mountains. The deacon hands me the communion plate covered with a dainty cloth. We bow to each other briefly. Then come two chalices. We bow again. The altar is appointed with beautiful but simple lace and some green details, reminding the congregation that we are in ordinary time.

I look out on our humble congregation. I see people from many nations—an old couple sitting near the front, a newly arrived family fleeing the economic disaster in Venezuela, venerable Filipino women who have lived in Madrid for decades, a smattering of children and babies, the Spanish man who many years ago was a Catholic monk. Many of the people who attend church are poor immigrants gathered from around the world. Some came here seeking work, while others were fleeing from man-made disasters in countries like Ukraine and Venezuela. Many are from a Catholic background; some folks from Romania and the Ukraine are most familiar with the rites of the Orthodox Churches. Some of the Spaniards have been Protestants since birth, their parents having converted in the days when not being Roman Catholic in Spain could mean no schooling for children or healthcare. Finally, we have a handful of evangelicals and Pentecostals from Latin America and elsewhere.

Sunday morning is our only communion service. We celebrate it every other Sunday, alternating with Morning Prayer. Usually we have about fifty people in attendance, though passersby often stick their heads in the door to see and hear what is going on. Some stay for a while, others make the sign of the cross and move on. The cathedral is in a busy neighborhood and the rumble of a car rolling by or the barking of a dog often wafts in. When we sing the antiphons and lauds it is to Spanish tunes accompanied by organ. While the words are ancient, the musical settings are taken from Spanish operatic music known as Zarzuela.

The cathedral is the oldest still-functioning Protestant church in Spain. Sunlight fills the sanctuary, flooding through stained-glass into the sanctuary. Yet, there is a strong Reformed feel to the space. The stained-glass windows do not depict any person or image, but simple geometrical patterns. All around the nave and over the altar the chief decorations are scripture verses painted in an archaic font in red and black exhorting us to "Rejoice always," and "Be always in prayer."

The liturgy used in the Reformed Episcopal Church of Spain (IERE are the Spanish initials) is the Mozarabic. In all the other parts of the Anglican Communion where I have been, and there have been many, the local church uses some version of the Book of Common Prayer that has an identifiable link to the old prayer books of England. Not so here. The Mozarabic liturgy, also called the Visigothic liturgy, is the old liturgy used by the Spaniards during the centuries of Islamic occupation (711–1492). When the founding fathers of the IERE were gathering, they decided to revive (and edit) this ancient Spanish worship service. They viewed the Roman Rite as a foreign liturgy imposed from outside of Spain and their desire was to return to the ancient Christianity of the Spanish people. The IERE officially became a member of the Anglican Communion in 1980, extra-provincial to the Archbishop of Canterbury, and so this Mozarabic Rite is an Anglican liturgy, albeit a rather complicated one, at least for me, an American Episcopal priest.

I didn't grow up in The Episcopal Church or really in any church for that matter. I was baptized as an infant at a Lutheran church in Montana, but my parents rarely took me to church. I didn't know anything about Christianity. Didn't know who Jesus was, didn't know that Christmas was about his birth or Easter about his resurrection. It wasn't until I was a teen living in Mexico that I really started to learn about Christianity after a friend from school invited me to a Bible church where his father was pastor. I was quite content with that conservative form of evangelical Christianity for many years, well into my days as a philosophy student at the University of Texas at San Antonio.

Then, I got engaged to Sharon. I was attending a large Bible church in San Antonio—one whose average weekend attendance is larger than many dioceses of The Episcopal Church. Sharon was attending an Evangelical Free church where her dad was one of the elders. We decided we needed to find a church together. The Bible church I was attending had become so enormous that we wanted something a bit more . . . not enormous. We also knew that at Sharon's church I'd always be the guy "dating Bob's daughter." My mentor from Intervarsity Christian Fellowship—an interdenominational ministry at our university—introduced me to the men's fellowship of Christ Episcopal Church in San Antonio. I played guitar for the men's retreat, and I later started playing guitar for the small Wednesday evening service. We decided to try Christ Church on a Sunday morning.

We were hooked. I loved all the Bible readings. It dawned on me how ironic it was that we read a lot more Bible in the Episcopal liturgy than at the Bible church. Sharon loved the Prayers of the People. We were not just praying for whatever specific need was pressing—healing, jobs, life decisions—but everything: the poor, the nations, government, church leaders. We also came to love the hymnal. These hymns had deep theological resonance; they were not the sappy, overly-emotional praise tunes we had become so accustomed to. We were confirmed in 2002 at Christ Church, married there in 2003, and have been serving as cross-cultural missionaries of that parish since 2004.

The next years of our life were lived in the Diocese of Jerusalem. While the diocese technically includes Lebanon and Syria, almost all its congregations are in Israel-Palestine and Jordan. After two years of studying Arabic in Jordan, I was invited to help found a seminary in Nazareth for the country's 5,000 or so Protestants. Nazareth is in Israel, but its population is Arab. The people of the city speak both Hebrew and Arabic, and both languages can be heard on the street. Our church there was *Kanisat al Masiih*, which means Christ Church or Church of the Messiah.

One day in 2015, I found myself in Fort Worth, Texas for business. A good friend of mine from middle school messaged me on Facebook. He was living in Fort Worth. We should get together, he said. We did and he shared his vision for planting a church in Madrid. Would Sharon and I pray about joining them? My friend and I had completed middle and high school together in Puebla,

Mexico, so we were both fluent in Spanish. I had never thought about moving to Spain, but in 2016, I came to Madrid with our daughter, Amelia, who was eight years old at the time. I was here to scout out the land. I spoke with educators, missionaries, and clergy. I had four things to offer: experience in church planting, evangelism, teaching at a seminary, and communicating the gospel to Muslims. I asked around—was the local church in need of these things? The answer was a resounding yes. Fast forward: we arrive in Madrid in August of 2017 with the blessing of our parish; our diocese, West Texas; and mission society, Anglican Frontier Missions; and with the sponsorship of the Episcopal Church of Spain.

Though I was already fluent in Spanish upon arriving here—thanks to those years in Mexico and my mother's side of the family, the Boteros, from Colombia—I was not prepared for the Mozarabic liturgy. It has about nineteen moveable parts: three Bible readings, the collect of the day, various antiphons and lauds, the proper preface, and more. One of the differences between the Mozarabic liturgy and what I was used to is when the table is set for communion: before the Prayers of the People.

While I set the table this particular Sunday, two congregants gather the offering. Meanwhile, the deacon hands me the bread and wine from the small credence table. Once the offerings of the congregation are brought forward a brief prayer of dedication is said and they are set aside. Then we say the Prayers of the People, followed by the Confession and Absolution. After the Absolution, the congregation, returning the favor, so to speak, says to the priest, "May God Almighty have mercy also on you and forgive you all your sins, and grant you eternal life, through Jesus Christ our Lord." Then follows the Peace. I turn to the servers and clasp their hands and say, "*La paz del Señor.*" The congregants turn to one another and shake hands while men kiss women on the cheeks. There is a general milling around during this time, and I scan the crowd to make sure to greet any new visitors in person.

After the Peace, I say what for most Episcopal priests would normally come immediately after setting the communion table.

I speak the words of institution in Spanish: "*En la noche en que fue entregado . . . .*" I pray that God would send the Holy Spirit upon the gifts of bread and wine and upon the congregation: "*Y te suplicamos humildemente, o Padre misericordioso, que por tu poderosa bondad te dignes bendecir y santificar para nuestro uso, con tu palabra y con tu Espíritu, estos dones y criaturas tuyas de pan y vino . . . .*" The congregation and clergy then say together a prayer dedicating ourselves, "*nos presentamos y te hacemos ofrenda de nosotros mismos, nuestras almas y nuestros cuerpos, como un sacrificio racional, santo y vivo, para ti.*" Then, after the Great Amen, and with the consecrated bread and wine still on the altar, the congregation stands to recite the Nicene Creed.

We then recite the Lord's Prayer according to our own, local custom, a litany of sorts:

The presider says, "Our Father, who art in Heaven, hallowed be thy name," and the people say, "Amen."

The presider continues, "Thy Kingdom come, thy will be done on earth as it is in heaven," and again the people say, "Amen."

The presider says, "Give us this day our daily bread," and the people respond, "For you are God."

The presider then says, "Forgive us our sins as we forgive those who sin against us," and the people say, "Amen."

Then the presider says, "And lead us not into temptation," and the people conclude, "But deliver us from evil. Amen."

During the liturgy, some foreign congregants look at the order of worship, trying to work through the Spanish, while others simply keep their eyes closed. But when we come to the Lord's Prayer, everyone lights up. Everyone knows the Lord's Prayer, and because of the poverty of so many of them, they really understand the supplication to give us our daily bread. The response from the congregation, "For you are God!" is always vigorous, sometimes thunderous.

After the Lord's Prayer, the bishop or sub-dean pronounces the great blessing over the people, and it is time for communion. There is no altar rail, so most people kneel on cushions that have been placed on the steps leading to the sanctuary. Two people administer the bread, and two people the wine (grape juice, actually). Once the six to eight people gathered at the steps have all communed, the bishop says a brief blessing over them or simply says, "Go in peace."

One day I asked our bishop, "Why do we set the table and *then* do most of the liturgy?" He explained that the historical purpose for this was to provide a "small catechesis" before taking communion. The original intention, according to him, was to make sure that people understood what they were doing and what the Christian faith was all about. Imagine setting a table and having everyone sit down for a special meal and saying, "Now before we eat, let's remember who we really are. Let's remember where this food comes from. Let's confess how we have been brought together in this place at this time."

The Sunday liturgy ingrains in us the gracious, ineffable scheme of God to pour out God's saving love for a world that has lamentably and with pronounced consistency turned its face away from God. It also can and should draw us into the vision of spreading blessing to those who did not work for it. I look up and see a man who fled his country: here, he has a community surrounding him, praying for him, that will help feed him, that will care for him and love him as best we can.

When it comes to God's grace, as Luther reminds us, "We are all beggars." Into our outstretched hands the crucified and risen Lord meets us in the bread of heaven and the cup of salvation. Beggars all of us: *Limosneros, mutasawwiliin, qabtsan.* How is it that I, an American Episcopal priest, a guy who grew up in Colorado and Puebla, Mexico, am sharing the Eucharist with God's people in Madrid? As their priest, no less? Me, most of all, how did I receive this blessing that I have not merited?

After communion, I hand the paten to the deacon, and then the chalices. The deacon places them on the credence table and covers them with a cloth. After some brief announcements and a post-communion prayer, we are finished. The clergy line up facing the bishop's cathedra, which is right behind the altar. We bow and, accompanied by a hymn, walk to the rear of the nave. It's time to shake hands and chat with visitors and parishioners before we go out, sharing a blessing we did not work for.

12

Dancing in Friendship with God

PAUL FROMBERG

I am never the first person to arrive at St. Gregory's on Sunday morning; someone always gets there ahead of me. "Good morning Paul!" Mark greets me when I walk into the building. "I just have one question for you . . . ." Unlike my experience in other congregations I have served, St. Gregory's does not expect that the rector will do everything. And there is a lot of work to be done before the Sunday liturgy begins: music books to place on chairs, chalices and patens to set on the altar, the Gospel book to be marked at the day's reading, oil lamps to fill and light, charcoal discs to light for the thuribles, guests and visitors to welcome. We give away a lot of work.

Saint Gregory of Nyssa Church was founded in 1978 with a charge to continue liturgical development in the direction that had been set out for the 1979 Book of Common Prayer, drawing directly on the classical resources for practices that would enhance congregational participation. St. Gregory's was to create a liturgy embodying an authentic Anglican approach, gaining from modern scholarship, open to new material, and yielding experience to serve the whole church. Our founders retired in 2007, and the congregation began a process that resulted in my call as rector in 2008.

St. Gregory's is made up of children and elders, families and singles, straight and gay people, lifelong Christians, interfaith couples, converts, skeptics, and seekers. Our patron saint, Gregory of Nyssa, a fourth-century bishop, inspires us with his vision of human life in friendship with God. We join in worship and service, creating a community that shares the unconditional welcome offered at Jesus's table. St. Gregory's is an intentional community open to all. We are dedicated to sharing the gospel through social engagement, liturgy, art, friendship, music, beauty, and dance. All of this happens whether or not I show up on a Sunday morning.

As the rector of the church, giving work away has been tremendously liberating. It has also required me to understand the relationship between congregation and priest in a new way. I was formed in professional ministry believing that I had certain privileges and responsibilities in the liturgy that nobody else could touch. Almost none of those were my canonical responsibilities; most were just the turf that I was taught to guard carefully. What we have discovered at St. Gregory's is that the core value of liturgical leadership—among the ordained and the non-ordained—is the giveaway. So a visitor who comes to our liturgy will see lots of people active in the service: lighting the lamps and candles, taking turns proclaiming the Scriptures, serving communion, speaking their own intercessions during the prayers, making coffee and cleaning up when it's time to go home. And we do this week after week after week, inviting first-time visitors to share the work with us. Because each person works to make church happen, our community recalls where its corporate identity and relationships are rooted: in the worship and praise of God shared freely with old friends and strangers.

God is known in the activity of making church happen. We place a premium on giving work away, letting people do things not because they have to, but because it is one way to know more about their life in God. People feel as if the work of the church is their own because it is. What I have discovered in sharing my authority with the members of the community is that my own work as a priest is enriched. I am free to give my job away in ways that amplify the work of God in our midst. As a result, our community is filled with people of all ages and stages of life who are competent as leaders. In this practice, there is both freedom and accountability—two very different phenomena.

Freedom has always been pretty easy for us at St. Gregory of Nyssa. We were started as an experimental center of liturgical innovation. The bishop of California gave us a massive amount of freedom in pushing the limits of the liturgy. Freedom was instilled in our culture from the beginning, as was creativity. And in the San Francisco Bay Area, people like the idea of those two things. But accountability has always been a challenge for us because it is a concept that operates on different levels. We are accountable to the diocese, to the bishop, to one another in community, and to our own particular charism as a congregation of Christ's church. And accountability is culturally dissonant in our location. People rarely RSVP to parties in the Bay Area, and if they do, they may or may not show up. Commitment, one side of accountability in relationship, is a position that seems to be always swimming upstream in our location. But we at St. Gregory's work hard at being accountable to one another. We find the energy to do this because of the love that is woven through our community, which is just another way of saying the experience of God is powerfully present.

The experience of God must come before any consideration of our freedom or accountability. More specifically, it is the love of God manifested in Jesus Christ that comes before anything else. And it is this love that is the urgent, pressing occasion that calls our community to live in love with one another. So, freedom and creativity—those things that St. Gregory's has very little trouble with—become more fruitful for us because they can only be exercised in the love that sets us free to serve one another and love one another in the community. And accountability—the thing that is harder for us—is fruitful because it is part and parcel of the love of Jesus we strive to experience. We follow the example of Jesus's love not just because it is good and noble, but also because we believe the love that Jesus showed us is the foundation of the world and our true nature. This is why we welcome people, the prepared and the unprepared, freely and openly to share everything that we have. And this intention is, literally, engraved on our altar table.

On the base of the altar, facing the main entrance to the church, is carved and gilded this verse (in Greek) from the fifteenth chapter of Luke's Gospel, "This guy welcomes sinners and dines with them." Jesus's opponents spoke these words as an insult and challenge to his honor. But Jesus *meant* to scandalize his contemporaries, sharing the table with the worthy and unworthy, the unprepared and the pious. This is the heart of the gospel. It is also the core meaning of St. Gregory's practice of eucharistic welcome. Just as Jesus welcomed all people to share his table, so we extend the same invitation to those who come to worship with us whether they are baptized or not. And although some say that this means we have a low opinion of baptism, nothing could be further from the truth. This is represented in another inscription on our altar.

Opposite the church's entrance, outside a set of tall glass doors, there is a rock sculpture over which water continually flows. This is the baptismal font. The orientation of the altar table and the font is intended to demonstrate our theological appreciation of the two dominical sacraments. First, we welcome everyone to receive the bread and wine, which are Christ's body and blood from the altar. Later, we encourage those who have not been baptized to receive the water, anointing, and laying on of hands of holy baptism. On the side of the altar, facing the font are carved these words from the seventh-century bishop and theologian Isaac of Nineveh, "Did not our Lord share his table with tax collectors and harlots? So then, do not distinguish between worthy and unworthy, all must be equal in your eyes to love and serve." These words indicate St. Gregory's baptismal theology. In baptism God prepares us to continue the work of Jesus, serving all people as Christ serves us. Those who are baptized take on the new humanity of Jesus Christ. We carry this identity wherever we go, dancing through the world in friendship with God.

Each Sunday, our liturgy concludes with congregational dance. While we sing the final hymn, we dance to a simple Greek-style folk dance, going around and around the altar table. Everyone is close to one another. The cantor gives instructions, a drummer keeps the rhythm, and everyone begins to move. Once everyone is moving in step, the whole assembly sings and dances together around the table. No one receives an explicit exemption from the dance. We never warn people to participate only if they feel comfortable. We assume that telling someone to do something only if they feel comfortable implies that what we will do is very uncomfortable. Those who wish to stand back and watch the dance are free to do so; chairs are always available for those who need them.

The expressions on people's faces during the dance range from bemusement to laughter to bliss. When we conclude, there is always laughter and sometimes applause from visitors. The experience of congregational dance puts everyone on the same level of vulnerability. The dismissal, the high point of energy in the liturgy, follows. People bring food and drink out for everyone to enjoy, placing it right on the altar so that we can continue our eucharistic fellowship.

What I'm learning about the world through my engagement with St. Gregory's is the tangible experience of God the Holy Trinity alive in our midst. Wherever we go, God goes with us; and wherever we go, God is there already. Every Sunday, this becomes clearer to me. Week by week, we are becoming strong to know and love—and trust—the God of Jesus Christ as the one who is making all things new. And week by week, we are being transformed into a new people.

13

The Sound of One Hand Clapping

MICHAEL BATTLE

The following is one of my favorite jokes. One Sunday morning, a mother goes upstairs to wake up her son. She tells him it is time to get ready for church.

He replies, "I'm not going."

"Why not?" she asks.

"I'll give you two good reasons," he says. "The first one is, they don't like me; and the second is, I don't like them."

His mother replies, "I'll give you two good reasons why you *should* go to church. First, you're fifty-three years old. And second, you're the priest."

For those of us called to be leaders in the church, this is biting humor. It bites not just because of the obvious stressors of leadership, but also because the childish rationalization for not going to church, "they don't like me and I don't like them," masks a deeper problem: we often stop worshipping God. And, as I have learned through my own experience, even for those of us who make it to church regularly, we often stop worshipping God there as well. Although I am an Episcopal priest and a theologian, this is a severe problem not just for clergy and academics. For many people today, lay and clergy alike, and perhaps especially and poignantly so for those of us who are in church every Sunday, we find ourselves confronted by, even afflicted by, the realization that at some point we stopped worshipping God.

In my ordained life in the church, I encounter the paradox of leading worship while simultaneously trying to worship God. This feels difficult, if not impossible, to do. I remember, while serving as chaplain to the House of Bishops of The Episcopal Church, the presiding bishop at that time, Frank Griswold, telling me about his own conundrum while leading worship. It was Sunday morning and as the acolytes processed down the nave of the church, a pair of them started chewing their gum to climax into some of the biggest bubbles Griswold had ever seen. The pure intention to worship the Lord can be burst as easily as so many chewing-gum bubbles. Leading worship and worshipping at the same time makes us face the reality that our gaze is oftentimes more easily fixed on the gum-chewing faces of acolytes than upon the face of our Lord. This is funny, but also serious because if I, the spiritual leader, am not worshipping God, I am a noisy gong and a clanging cymbal. This is a problem not just for clergy, but also for many in our spiritually diseased society who are so consumed with consuming and distracted by trivia that they no longer really trust in God even as we continue to profess belief in God in high numbers. I think here of the Zen riddles that ask things like, "What is the sound of one hand clapping?" These paradoxical questions help us unravel deeper truths about ourselves and our world where seemingly impossible opposites appear to cancel each other out. On Sunday mornings I ponder another riddle: how do we lead worship and worship God at the same time?

My response is to ask another question: how does one practice worship when all along worship is something that God does in us? This question confronts me with the difficult matter of discerning what I am doing when I worship God. Am I a dispenser of information? During worship, I usually have to direct folks to where God is—"We will use Eucharistic Prayer A, found on page 361 in the Book of Common Prayer." Am I a counselor? I usually serve in this way right before Sunday worship in order to allay everyone's anxieties about where to stand, who is absent, and why the heat isn't working in the church. Am I a coach? I sound like an NFL coach on Sunday mornings telling acolytes to flair out to the right. Am I a teacher? On any given Sunday, I explain the teachings of Jesus from the pulpit.

Perhaps I am thinking about the question the wrong way round. Parker Palmer's reflections on the experience of mentoring and mutuality are helpful. He says,

> I ask the question that opens to the deeper purpose of this exercise: not "What made your mentor great?" but "What was it about you that allowed great mentoring to happen?" Mentoring is a mutuality that requires more than meeting the right teacher: the teacher must meet the right student. In this encounter, not only are the qualities of the mentor revealed, but the qualities of the student are drawn out in a way that is equally revealing.[1]

With Palmer's insight, I begin to make sense of how to worship as well as to lead worship. I need to enter the mystery of how Jesus enables us to participate in the triune love of God. From all eternity Christ lives in mutual relationships of fellowship and freedom with the Father and the Holy Spirit. In the incarnation of the Word, the boundless love of the triune God revealed in the

---

1. Palmer, *The Courage to Teach*, 21.

humanity of Jesus draws us into God's way of life in solidarity with sinners, the oppressed, and with all of creation. Jesus glorifies the Father through the power of the Spirit by allowing the Father to be glorified in him. This is the pattern for worship that Jesus sets for us: we glorify God by allowing God to be glorified in us. Since Jesus was human like us in every way, except without sin, I suspect that means Jesus had the same problems in worship that we all do, although maybe he didn't have the distraction of bubble gum. In this there is the hope that even our halting worship can be healed.

So, how does one practice worship when all along worship is something that God does in us? The answer is found in realizing that when we worship God we ultimately depend upon the Holy Spirit to lead the worship in us. As St. Paul teaches us, at the end of the day, *God* is the only one who truly prays (Rom 8:26–28). So, in a true sense, worship is *happening to us*, in spite of ourselves. Jesus modeled all of this as he, too, faced the distractions and transference of expectations by others. Especially as Jesus displays the conundrum of God praying to God, we can learn something that can help us understand how we lead worship and worship God at the same time.

Jesus invites all of us—not just clergy—to realize that simply by being attentive to one another we participate in how God happens to us. In other words, Jesus teaches us that worship is always about mutuality. From such insight I realize I cannot yell at the acolytes because Jesus taught me they are God's children. Jesus teaches us how to worship in that the goal of human life is participation in the self-giving love of God. I need to learn how to see in ordinary human frustration that God is present. By learning to be more mutual with one another, God facilitates the revelation of true worship. This revelation honors those who innately know that God is known through vulnerability. This is counterintuitive, however, because we often think worship is our responsibility, something we do. I have grown to understand that worshipping God is more about making room for God than my doing something for God.

My goal now on Sunday mornings is to be as authentic as I am on Monday to Saturday mornings. By doing so, my understanding of worship shifts from an individualistic experience into a social movement. This should help us with Martin Luther King, Jr.'s scathing prophetic critique that eleven o'clock on Sunday morning is the most segregated hour in the United States. Embracing a deeper understanding of worship can help us with our social complexities as well as our spiritual malaise. If worship is about participation in the self-giving love of the triune God that liberates and creates new life, then that means we must also share in God's solidarity with the vulnerable and God's hope for the whole creation. Such an embrace echoes what Michael Gungor, a progressive, white, contemporary Christian singer, sang about; namely, "God is not a white man."[2] Such spiritual convictions need not lead to civil wars but should actually help to sustain authentic faith in the living God rather than our vapid idols. I have grown to value the Anglican/Zen balance between the theory and practice of worship because now I understand that when it comes to worship, ordinary things matter to God. The acolyte blowing bubble gum bubbles in church matters to God. Human things matter to God. Being black matters to God. When worshipping the God revealed in Jesus, we learn that we cannot love God whom we have not seen if we hate people we do see.

As an African American, Christian theologian, I argue that how I continue to see "what is not there" is informed by my commitment to God's interrelational life as Trinity. From this perspective of God's mutuality I too must practice "what is not there," namely, true worship. This reminds me of Frederick Buechner's definition of vocation. Those who worship God have an opportunity to develop "the place where your deep gladness and the world's deep hunger meet." By being mutual with people sitting in the pew on Sunday morning (and maybe even laughing with the bubble-gum-blowing acolyte), I also facilitate the revelation of what true worship is—loving God and loving our neighbor as

2. It is interesting that Gungor experienced an onslaught of criticism for stating such an obvious fact.

ourselves. Instead of our liberal and conservative wars that look the same at eleven o'clock on Sunday morning as they do when Congress is in session, we will do better by seeing worship as mutuality in the life of the triune God.

Seeing worship as both our attention to God and to God's creation helps us move beyond Sunday morning. In other words, learning how to pray makes us better people. Our patience increases. I want to get out of bed and go to church on Sunday morning. I realize now that it is often only after a long, fruitless effort that ends in despair, when we can no longer expect anything in worship, that, from outside ourselves, God makes the gift of each other come as a marvelous surprise. It is through these efforts of attending to how God happens to us through each other that we participate in the profound effects of worshipping God. When we truly show up on Sunday we destroy the false sense of fullness by acknowledging our need for God and each other. When we worship, we also acknowledge that we are not the ultimate being— God is.

I learned this first hand in 1993 and 1994 when I lived in residence with Archbishop Desmond Tutu in Cape Town, South Africa. Living with Tutu shaped my vocation to have its current trajectory of being a professor and Episcopal priest. Primary to this formation, however, was the privilege of worshipping God with Tutu. In so doing I learned in those days how a Christian on the world's stage not only survives the stress of being a voice for the voiceless but also thrives in the meantime. Tutu's habits of both saying his prayers as well as meaning them made a imprint on me. Parker Palmer is right to ask, "What was it about you that allowed great mentoring to happen?" Well, for me, I was ready to learn how to worship God and lead others to do the same. My daily life of saying my prayers with Tutu enabled me to see that I cannot be a Christian alone. We are authentically human to the extent that we belong, we participate, and we share, as Tutu has said. And as I have learned, this is perhaps especially so in the mutuality of belonging, participating, and sharing in worship together.

Here's one of my favorite stories of unknown origin that speaks to the importance of praying with others. An elderly man stopped going to church. After a few weeks, the pastor paid a visit and she found the man at home alone, sitting in front of a fire. The man led her to a comfortable chair near the fireplace. She made herself at home but said nothing. After some silent minutes, she stood up and went over to the fireplace and took the fire tongs. She carefully picked up a brightly burning ember and placed it to one side, alone. She sat back in her chair, still silent. They both watched all this in quiet contemplation. Then, the isolated ember flickered and diminished. Soon it was cold and lifeless. She glanced at her watch and realized it was time to leave. Before she reached the door, she picked up the dead ember and placed it back in the middle of the fire. Immediately it began to glow again. With a tear running down his cheek, the man said, "Thank you for the fiery sermon. I will be back in church next Sunday."

Bibliography

Palmer, Parker. *The Courage to Teach: Exploring the Inner Landscape of a Teacher's Life*. San Francisco: Jossey-Bass, 1998.

14

Being Remembered in the Liturgy

BJ HEYBOER

"Out of the depths have I called to you, O LORD."

These are the opening words of Psalm 130. They are also the words Andy Catlett hears in his memory, spoken in his grandmother's voice.

Andy, a farmer and agricultural journalist, is the main character in a brief novel by Wendell Berry entitled, *Remembering*. Those opening words of the psalm wash over him in the midst of an excruciating chapter in his life. It's a chapter in which Andy feels cut off from his family and friends, from the land he loves, indeed—from himself.

And here's why: early in the novel, we learn that Andy and two others were helping a neighbor harvest corn. It was getting late in the day, and Andy, Nathan, Danny, and Jack still had a fair amount of field left to cover. The corn picker jammed, and Andy stopped to clear the machine, leaving it running.

Berry writes,

> He began pulling the crammed stalks out of the machine, irritated by the delay. He pulled them out one at a time, shucked the ears that were on them, and threw the stalks aside. And then something happened that he thought he had imagined but, as it turned out, had not imagined at all: The machine took his hand. Of course, he knew he must have given the hand, but it was so quickly caught he could almost believe that the machine had leapt for it. While his mind halted, unable to come to the fact, his body fended for itself, braced against the pull, and held. When intelligence lighted in him again, he saw that only the hand was involved, and he carefully shifted his feet so as to give himself more leverage against the rollers; he did not want his jacket sleeve to be caught. And he was already yelling—"Hey! Hey!"—trying to pitch his voice above the noise of the machine. There is no way for him to know how long he held out against the pull of the rollers, which soon pulled with less force, for they were lubricated with his blood.[1]

That day Andy lost his right hand. But the hand wasn't all he lost. He lost his identity. He lost his sense of self as a farmer, his sense of worth as a neighbor, and his unique ability to be a tender lover to his wife—the woman he longed to reach for and hold as he had before. In short, Andy Catlett lost himself.

In Berry's beautiful story, Andy journeys thousands of miles—geographically, emotionally, relationally, and spiritually—in search of healing for all that has been crushed and cut off in him. On his travels, it dawns on Andy how his identity is bound up with that of his family members, friends, and neighbors. Calling out from the depths of alienation, he realizes that to be made whole

---

1. Berry, *Remembering*, 11–12.

again, he must give himself—including his broken body—to the community to which he belongs.

My story is not nearly as dramatic as Andy's. In my twenty years as an Episcopalian and my relatively short tenure as an ordained priest, I have not suffered the devastating loss of my right hand—or any other visible body part, for that matter. But in the context of corporate weekly worship, I am reminded time and time again of how my identity is bound up with the people of God to whom I belong—and who belong to me. By grace, I remember who I am—and who we are together—through the liturgy of The Episcopal Church. Or rather, the liturgy re-members me with others to God.

There are three particular chapters in my story that best illustrate how the liturgy has remembered me in my journey thus far. The first chapter takes place two decades ago when I was introduced to The Episcopal Church.

I moved from Michigan to the Chicago suburbs to begin a new job in publishing. Having grown up in the Reformed tradition, I looked for a church whose worship was familiar—a source of recognition and comfort in the midst of so much in my life that was strange and unknown. I worshiped at that church with several hundred people week after week. I joined a Bible study, and volunteered in a ministry for children whose parents were divorced. But in spite of my consistent participation in the life of that church, Sunday worship left me feeling cut off. Perhaps due the size of the church, I was regarded consistently as a stranger in worship, unrecognizable to others. Many months passed, until one day a greeter asked me, "Oh, what brings you here today?" I thought, "The same thing that has brought me here every other Sunday for the last six months." I felt alienated and alone, despite being in the presence of so many people.

A few months later, friends invited me to join them for worship on Good Friday at their parish, St. Barnabas Episcopal Church in Glen Ellyn. Little did I realize then that the deep remembrance of our Lord's death that evening would be what, liturgically speaking, brought me back to life.

Several things stand out in my memory of worship that night, particularly the physical participation of people in the liturgy. But what I remember most was the veneration of the cross. As a small choir sang, "Sing, My Tongue, the Glorious Battle," people reverently began to make their way up the aisle. At the start of the third verse, I felt compelled to stand.

> He endures the nails, the spitting,
> vinegar, and spear, and reed;
> from that holy body broken
> blood and water forth proceed:
> earth, and stars, and sky, and ocean,
> by that flood from stain are freed.[2]

As the choir continued to sing, I silently moved forward and knelt before the cross with others making obeisance there. Tears streamed from my eyes, splashed down my cheeks, and discovered a new home on the wood. Extending my right hand, I tenderly reached for the cross, stooping to offer a kiss.

That night I experienced a powerful sense of being re-membered in the drama of worship. With the exception of three people, I did not know anyone in that sacred space. But I felt like I belonged to God with them in a profound way. I participated in the liturgy with my whole being: hands, feet, legs, knees, ears, voice, lips, tears, body, mind, and spirit. In the silence of deep remembrance, I was recognized as a daughter of God and welcomed by others as a living member of Christ's body. I had found my home in The Episcopal Church.

A second memorable chapter in my story of being remembered by the liturgy occurred a few years after that Good Friday. I had moved back to Michigan and settled in with my new liturgical community, St. Andrew's Episcopal Church in Grand Rapids. But ordinary activities at that time in my life became overwhelming, a crushing weight overshadowed me, and darkness descended not only on my nights, but also on my days. Doctors and

---

2. Church Publishing, *The Hymnal 1982*, #166.

counselors diagnosed my heavy heart and treated me for anxiety and depression.

I experienced the liturgy as I did much of life during that time: as rather subdued and a bit dim. But because the liturgy remembered me—no matter how I felt—I found it a source of strength, healing, and restoration. On the days I couldn't sing, the voices of others carried me. When I struggled to say, "I believe," the profession of faith by my sisters and brothers bolstered and sustained me. Like Andy Catlett trying to figure out who he was without his right hand, I was searching for a new way to sing and speak and be who I was in light of my loss and struggle. I am certain that I would not have been able to locate myself so fully again without God's grace and the healing power of my beloved worshiping community.

The third and final chapter in this story of being remembered in and by the liturgy has unfolded just in the last few years since my ordination. I am currently the priest of two small rural Michigan parishes, and along with the change of vocation and roles, now I occupy a different physical position and space in worship than I did as a layperson.

From where I stand on Sunday mornings, I face the gathered body as I pray, preside, partake, speak, and listen. When my eyes sweep across the assembly, the people and I exchange not only words of dialog, but also silent glances of recognition—some that express volumes, and others that defy distinct interpretation. There is the man who just lost his job, and the woman who has been diagnosed with cancer but has not made it public yet. I see the kid who is back to school—and I recall how much he hates school. Their presence and participation play a prominent part in our worship of God, for the liturgy—though structured—is living and breathing. It is infused with the presence of the resurrected Lord; additionally, our worship takes a unique expression each week depending on the people who are there. Call it our collective energy or spirit: I am keenly aware from where I stand that the people who are present—and the geographical, emotional, relational, and spiritual routes they have taken to get there—play a role in the liturgy of word and sacrament. Together, we are remembered as the body of Christ, gathered to glorify God.

One of the beautiful things of serving in small parishes is that I am aware of who is not present as well. I have no desire to make people feel guilty for not being in church on any given Sunday; I just long for them to know that I have a keen sense of the so-called Ubuntu philosophy as it pertains to worship: I am who I am because of who we are together. Through the liturgy, we are knit together. And while God's church transcends time and space, it is good to be gathered together and be remembered as one body on Sunday mornings in Newaygo County.

The remembering I experience as priest in the liturgy also takes place in my body. In chanting, preaching, and particularly in presiding at the altar, I experience within me an iota of the weight of what's happening in worship. For example, before beginning the *Sursum corda*, I have to literally set myself in position. I plant my feet, bend my knees, and adjust my hips—much like a batter at the plate getting ready to receive a pitch. I do this not because I think I'm going to hit some kind of liturgical home run, but because I feel the need to brace myself for the intensity of what comes next. With my lower body grounded, I raise my arms and hands, lifting up my heart and inviting others to do the same. Week after week, my body returns to this position, physically braced for a transforming encounter with the Risen Lord in the mystery of Holy Eucharist.

In the context of the Episcopal liturgy, I continue to encounter the living God with the people to whom I belong and who belong to me. Together, by grace, we are remembered once again as the people God has created us to be, strengthened and renewed to speak a word of wholeness and love to others who may be calling out from the depths, reaching for a hand.

Bibliography

Berry, Wendell. *Remembering: A Novel*. Berkeley: Counterpoint, 2008.

Church Publishing. *The Hymnal 1982, according to the Use of The Episcopal Church*. 1982 edition. New York: Church Pension Fund, 1985.

15

How the Book of Common Prayer Kept Me in the Family of Faith

IAN S. MARKHAM

It was at King's College London that I discovered and fell in love with Anglican liturgy. I was twenty years old. Here I was an undergraduate in a college where the Faculty in Theology and Religious Studies would stretch, pull, and question the students, yet would also gather to participate in the Daily Office or celebrate at the Eucharist.

Leslie Houlden, my favorite New Testament professor, was faithful; he was often present in chapel. Yet he was also one of the so-called "seven against Christ"—a contributor to *The Myth of God Incarnate*. I was puzzled by how this distinguished progressive New Testament scholar could participate fully in the traditional Morning Office, almost all of which was Scripture. How could he read the words of Scripture in worship yet constantly question the words of Scripture in his scholarship?

I was puzzled, but also exhilarated. A new world was opening up to me. One can be inside the family of faith, and, at the same time, be a questioning Christian. One can read and love Scripture and also read the text with a critical mind. It was this Anglican ethos, grounded in the Book of Common Prayer, that enabled me to stay inside the family of faith.

Some background is necessary. In 1962, I was born into what others call, "The Exclusive Brethren." This movement had its roots in the nineteenth-century sect known as the Plymouth Brethren, who in the 1940s had a schism over the issue of the autonomy of the local assembly. Two different groups were formed. The so-called "Open Brethren" wanted each assembly to have its own jurisdiction over local membership, while John Nelson Darby (1800–1882) insisted that all assemblies should "be of one heart, one mind, and one spirit." Therefore, the so-called "Darbyites" insisted all assemblies should recognize a national leadership—namely, the leadership of J. N. Darby. This was the seed of the Exclusive Brethren.

By 1962, the Exclusives were a small fundamentalist group, committed to separation from the world and expecting the rapture any day. Darby was the inventor of dispensationalism and with it the rapture. Over time, the restrictions had gradually increased. Contact with the outside world should be kept to an absolute minimum. Television and radio were forbidden. No one outside the assembly was permitted to enter our home nor could we visit their houses. After all, 2 John 10 was clear, "Do not receive into the house or welcome anyone who comes to you and does not bring this teaching." Therefore, I never attended a birthday party of a school friend; I had to eat apart from the rest of the children at school; we did not observe Christmas nor Easter (both were inherited pagan festivals); and all civic organizations were forbidden. Higher education was forbidden (education was limited to that required by the law of the land). We did loads of church. On Sunday, worship would start at 6 a.m. (after all, Mary was "up early" to seek her resurrected Lord), and that would be followed by a further four meetings (9 a.m., 12 noon, 3 p.m., and 6 p.m.).

This small world was our entire universe. There were no competing voices or alternatives to consider. Chances are this would have been my future, but for my father running into a major problem with the prohibition on civic organizations. Legislation was introduced in the late 1960s that required all pharmacists to be members of the Pharmaceutical Society. (My father was trained prior to the restrictions on graduate education.) He stopped practicing as a pharmacist and attempted to become a supplier of chemist sundries to pharmacy shops. With six children to feed, he realized that he was not earning enough to support his family; bankruptcy was looming. He was between a rock and a hard place; both bankruptcy and membership in the Pharmaceutical Society were incompatible with membership in the Exclusive Brethren.

My parents agonized. Then my father took the brave decision to leave. I remember being with him as he called his siblings. The consequences were brutal. As a family, every single person that we knew in the universe would never speak to us again. For the Exclusives, those who had "seen light and then rejected it" are most condemned. No one would have any contact with us. Sure enough, apart from one letter from his brother (who appealed to him to repent), my father has not heard from or seen any of his relatives since that time.

In our family, the Exclusives' worldview lingered for many more years. After all, my parents had been in the Exclusives for over forty years. They were still persuaded of the dangers of the world, the apostasy of the mainline churches, and of the fact that we are living in the last days. For a time, we lived in the twilight world of ex-members of the Exclusives. We would meet in the home of another former member for the breaking of the bread on Sunday morning. Then we found an Open Brethren assembly, which was very conservative. These ostensibly "open brethren" were opposed to all ecumenical projects, had strict expectations of behavior, and continued to teach and stress an apocalyptic worldview. It was in this environment, at the age of twelve, that I became a boy preacher.

Education does burst narrow worldview bubbles. In high school, I was introduced to the critical reading of the Bible. I was persuaded that biblical inerrancy was implausible and unlikely to be true. And then in my late teens, my mother fell ill and started the journey to her death. Cancer was the killer. My faith lay in tatters: intellectually, it did not make sense and, emotionally, I could not see any grace in the death of my mother.

So here I was at King's College London. And the liturgy started to repair my life. For years, I had disparaged the scripted prayers that seemed to deny the agency of the Holy Spirit. Slowly I discovered the Holy Spirit had been completely involved when those prayers were originally written down. I found the rhythm of the liturgy deeply powerful. I had been very critical that it was the same thing every service. But then the liturgy started going inside. C. S. Lewis got it right when he explained what a worshipper wants out of a service:

> They go to *use* the service, or, if you prefer, to *enact* it. Every service is a structure of acts and words through which we receive a sacrament, or repent, or supplicate, or adore. And it enables us to do these things best—if you like, it "works" best—when, through long familiarity, we don't have to think about it. As long as you notice, and have to count, the steps, you are not yet dancing but only learning to dance. A good shoe is a shoe you don't notice. Good reading becomes possible when you need not consciously think about eyes, or light, or print, or spelling.

> The perfect church service would be one we're almost
> unaware of; our attention would have been on God.[1]

I would sit through Morning Prayer; I attended the Eucharist. I learned the service inside out. It became a frame of reference where I could pray, cry, and think in the presence of God. The tradition was always front and center. I knew the Bible; and I loved the fact that Scripture was central. The sermon was not doing the heavy lifting of the service; for the Office, it was the canticles; for the Eucharist, it was The Great Thanksgiving. It became a perfectly fitting shoe. I also knew where I was in the liturgy, even if a word or phrase had triggered a "zoned out" moment where I offered some agony deep inside of me to God. The liturgy was providing God with some space to work on my fragile mind and life. God was bringing some healing to the vulnerable twenty-two-year-old.

Intellectually, the liturgy became a foil and conversation partner. One gift of the Exclusive Brethren upbringing is that the sense of God was inescapable. Just after my mother died, I tried desperately to be an atheist, but within weeks realized that was impossible because I was still praying. A sense of God has been the gift of my religious upbringing. Yet I needed liberation from the intolerance, cruelty, and intellectual vacuity of the Exclusives. Over the next thirty years, I needed the liturgy to represent the tradition. The incarnation was always important: an adequate theodicy needed the incarnate God to know the depth of suffering and pain. And you cannot have an incarnation without a Trinity. So fairly quickly, for this new Anglican, the basics of the faith were in place. Yet one's understanding of Scripture, angels, demons, the resurrection, sacraments, the priesthood—these were oft-visited questions within the context of the liturgy.

As I've aged, the witness of the liturgy is winning. Increasingly, I affirm the words in The Great Thanksgiving, "Therefore we praise you, joining our voices with Angels and Archangels and with all the company of heaven, who for ever sing this hymn to proclaim the glory of your Name." A multiplicity of spiritual entities and

1. Lewis, *Letters to Malcolm*, 4.

the witness of the communion of the saints make more and more sense to me. Yet I defend resolutely those who are not there. The image of the faith journey makes considerable sense. I need to be part of a community in which I can bring my doubts, struggles, and questions. At different times of my life, I have struggled with aspects of the Christian drama. The liturgy should not be changed to accommodate these moments; instead each person should be invited to function within the liturgy and trust that the narrative of the church can accommodate these important moments of skepticism and doubt. I want both Bishop John Shelby Spong and Bishop Tom Wright to be in the church, both participate in the same liturgy, and both be respected as part of the broad umbrella of Anglicanism.

The result is the distinctive Anglican ethos. Our liturgy represents the best of the past. And within the liturgy, God has space to heal, help, and illuminate. Finding the Book of Common Prayer was a life-changing gift; it was the vehicle that God used to save my faith. For that, I am eternally grateful.

Bibliography

Lewis, C. S. *Letters to Malcolm: Chiefly on Prayer*. New York: Harcourt, Brace, & World, 1963.

16

Ordinary Time

KIM EDWARDS

I hurry across a busy road, bells pealing through the summer air. The Episcopal church on the other side of the street is beautiful, built of gray stone. It looks like the church in rural England where my grandfather grew up, ringing the bells in the tower every Sunday as a boy.

Although I have passed this church hundreds of times on my way into town, I have never been inside. I am here this morning because people from the Presbyterian church I've been attending for the past few years have signed up to visit as part of a church exchange. I am not a part of this group, and so I am not really late. But all week I have been remembering the Episcopal church of my childhood, its rituals and rhythms, the deep sense of mystery I always felt, invisible but present, just beyond the patterns of the service and the social conventions. This morning, on an impulse, I decide to go.

The choir is gathering in the vestibule when I enter, shafts of colored light falling on their rustling white robes. I slip past them and slide into a pew near the back. The Presbyterians are already gathered on the other side, half-way up the aisle, consulting their bulletins and glancing around. People are arriving, seeking seats, standing or kneeling, genuflecting or crossing themselves. Candles are flickering on the altar; the stained-glass windows, a century old and vibrant, glow against the stone.

The procession begins. We all stand to sing as the verger leads the acolyte carrying the cross, the choir, and the clergy to the front, where they fan out into the chancel. I wonder what the Presbyterians are thinking. It's all so different from the church we attend, which has clear glass windows, Bibles in every pew, and a high soft light filling the white walls. Presbyterian prayers are written each week by the pastor and vary by church. Today however, we are praying the same prayers, at roughly the same time, as every other Anglican in the world. There is a shuffling of pages as the Presbyterians put down their hymnals and leaf through the red-covered Book of Common Prayer.

I grew up in The Episcopal Church, so all this is familiar, though I'm looking around, as well. I have not been to an Episcopal service in years and there are many changes. At this service female priests, still unusual in my childhood, outnumber the male priests. Some congregants are dressed quite formally with suits and hats and heels, but others are wearing shorts and sandals. Some people stand for prayers. Gluten-free wafers are available at the pulpit station, according to the bulletin. Two rows ahead, a same-sex couple links hands.

All the same, the gestures and rituals come flooding back to me, memory held in the body all these years, as if I've picked up a long-forgotten instrument and my fingers still remember all the notes. The Episcopal Church uses all the senses. Episcopalians embody the rituals of worship, a powerful key to memory. As I kneel and stand, sing and pray, my voice melds with a hundred other voices, and time falls away. I am here now, yes, in the middle of my life, married, a writer and professor and the mother of two daughters, officially a Presbyterian. Yet the child and teenager I once was is also present, daydreaming or singing in the choir, an acolyte touching the flame of my candle to the candles on the altar, chafing at all the rules and also worried about breaking them, and at the same time secretly grateful for steady rituals at a time in my life when so much seems chaotic and uncertain.

The gifts of God for the people of God. The priest lifts the elements and I am suddenly, inexplicably, moved. The communion rituals of both the Presbyterian and Episcopal Churches are holy sacraments, profoundly sacred moments. Still, for me the experiences are also very different. The Presbyterian loaf of bread on the Lord's table is not the perfect sphere of the host, suspended for a moment above the chalice at the altar. Tiny cups of grape juice on a metal tray, passed from hand to hand, don't hold the same symbolic power for me as the chalice, tipping as mouth after mouth touches the rim of a mystery.

Perhaps it is the connection to my childhood church. Perhaps it is the power of the service, or the idea of transformation, so much more vividly expressed through these Episcopal rites. Whatever the source, as the usher pauses at my pew and I walk up to the altar, my sense of timelessness increases. I know that this moment is connected to my past, and also to my future. Though it will take me several months, I will find my way back to this beautiful church where, for a few minutes every Sunday, I will understand in the deepest way that there is no such thing as ordinary time.

I am eight years old, wearing a dark blue cape lined with white that my mother made for me for Easter, running down the hallway from the Sunday school rooms, which have high windows and smell of paste, to the children's chapel, which is dim and solemn. I am not supposed to run here, in the basement of the church, that's one rule, and I'm laughing too loudly, breaking another rule, too. The Sunday school teachers, all women wearing dresses and heels, their hair well coifed, hush us. Outside the cold spring sunshine falls on the lake, the wet green grass. Inside the children's chapel we fall silent, concerned with getting everything right and remembering all the rules.

The children's chapel is the domain of women and children, though it was built by my grandfather, who emigrated from England and started a successful lumber business. He also constructed the beautiful parish hall overlooking the lake where coffee hours are held, another domain of women. Women in my childhood church sing in the choir but are seldom lectors, and at age eight I've never seen a woman priest. This seems to be a rule about how the church works, too, largely unspoken but clearly visible. It is organized like my family, where authority and power always reside with men.

I am the oldest daughter of the second son in a family where patterns of primogeniture were handed down from one generation to another. Although my grandfather loved me, I also knew in a deep intuitive way that I would never matter as much to him as my cousin, born a few weeks after I was, the oldest son of the oldest son.

Thus, being in the children's chapel is confusing to me. On one hand, my grandfather built this room and so my family is intrinsically connected to this quiet place of worship, and this feels like a good and special thing. On the other hand, I am a girl, a fact that diminishes and excludes me from full participation in this place, and that does not feel like a good thing at all.

Also confusing are the complex social hierarchies. Some very wealthy people attend this church; they, and their children, seem to be more important than everyone else. This is unstated, of course, but so clear to me as a child that for a long time I think that the Book of Common Prayer is a book for common people, of which I am one; for years I imagine there is another book for members of our church who matter more.

The rector, who was a journalist and not a politician before he became a priest, has perhaps tried to address some of this. In a sermon he pointed out that Jesus was, technically, illegitimate, and would have been seen as such by the people of his time and place. This so offended one of the pillars of the church, whose own unmarried son had just fathered a child, that he began a serious quest to oust the rector. For most of my youth we talk about forgiveness and the love of God during the worship service, followed immediately by the coffee hour, where there is urgent, whispered gossip about the rector and the move to kick him out.

Yet despite this tension and confusion, I am drawn to the church. I love being an acolyte, carrying the candles solemnly down the aisle and lighting the candles on the altar. I sense something compelling beyond the fixed structures of family and culture and tradition, beyond all the formality and hierarchies and rules. A quietness, and in that silence, beyond that silence, a mystery.

No one talks about this mystery, though, this stillness. I don't know how to put it into words, and anyway I would be afraid to speak. One day I inadvertently shut down a confirmation class by asking the wrong question: our textbook describes Jesus as being angry because the children are not allowed to come to him. But isn't anger a sin? I ask. I am not being a smart aleck—it is a serious question. The rector looks at me for a long moment before he announces abruptly that class is over. My face is flaming as we shuffle out. I have learned nothing about Jesus and anger, but I have learned in church to keep my questions to myself.

I am a writer even then, though mostly I am still writing bad poetry, and if anyone had pointed out that the word *spirit* is the root of the word *inspiration*, and that both are connected to the word for *breath*, I would have paid attention. I would have been all ears if anyone had drawn, as Evelyn Underhill does in her classic text *Mysticism*, a connection between the creation of art and its source:

> the work of art always owes its inception to some sudden
> uprush of intuitions of ideas for which the superficial self

cannot account; its execution to powers so far beyond the control of that self, that they seem, as their owner sometimes says, to "come from beyond." This is "inspiration"; the opening of the sluices, so that those waters of truth in which all life is bathed may rise to the level of consciousness.[1]

No one discusses this kind of thing, however. I turn eighteen and start college. Going to church begins to seem like just another arbitrary rule, one I can discard. And so, I do. I quit going to church. At the time, this feels to me like freedom.

It is an early evening, early spring. I am sitting in a circle in the library of this beautiful Episcopal church on a busy street, dwelling on a moment that was once far off in my future. There are six or seven of us gathered here, all ages and backgrounds, and no one is concerned with social hierarchies or superficial rules of dress. The priest reads a brief opening prayer. We close our eyes as a bell sounds, light and fading through the room, and then we sit silently for thirty minutes in centering prayer, letting go of the thoughts that distract us, entering the silence, learning to be still. When the bell sounds again we will stand up and make our way outside in silence, too, present to each other and yet respectful of the quiet that connects us. We meet weekly to do this, an anchoring ritual of prayer in a turbulent world.

The shelves of this library are full of books—theology, yes, and prayer books, and also novels and books of poetry and books about music and art. Books that ask difficult and interesting questions. I like having them surround us. It was through books like this that I first started finding my way back, not only to church, but to the sense I'd had as a child of a mystery just behind everything we did. I read the poet Kathleen Norris and her explorations of monastic life, and Marilynne Robinson's fiction, her characters alive with a sense of the presence in which we live and move and have our being. I discovered a deeper appreciation for the Bible, too. It is a living text, distinct from other texts, and it is also literature.

1 Underhill, *Mysticism*, 63.

The truths of Scripture are embedded in stories and poems, and because of this they cannot be reduced to a rule book or easy slogans, they cannot be quantified or contained. They meet each of us where we are at that moment in our lives. People who practice Lectio Divina sometimes talk about being read by Scripture—the stories and poems appeal to the senses and invite us into a deeper reality in the same way that Episcopal worship does. As a lector on Sunday mornings, I am often struck by the power of Scripture as I read, aware that in every Anglican church around the world the same words are being spoken, a deeper reality breaking through and connecting all who listen.

There is a steady comfort in this universality, in the familiar order of the Episcopal service. In stepping down from the lectern to take my seat, in the Prayers of the People and the passing of the Peace, in the stream of worshipers to the front of the church for Holy Communion, in this space where physical and mystical reality are so clearly intertwined.

Go in peace, to love and serve the Lord. This is the deacon's charge each week as we leave the church and re-enter our unpredictable lives. It's tempting to understand this charge as I did when I was young, to believe that we're being asked to somehow apply the order of worship to the chaotic, messy, and often painful world we encounter when we leave. But this world is God's creation, too, and it is not static. It is ever-evolving in ways we cannot begin to comprehend, and so are we, each one of us, growing toward completion. The deacon's farewell charge is not telling us what to do, I realize now, but rather it is teaching us how to relate. We are to go out into the world to love and serve God, who is already there, a living presence seeking not to impose a rigid order, but rather to transform the world, and all of us, through the radical mystery of love.

Bibliography

Underhill, Evelyn. *Mysticism: A Study in the Nature and Development of Spiritual Consciousness.* New York: Dutton, 1911.

17

Finding Home

Luisa E. Bonillas

Padre Nuestro Que estas en el cielo. I am flooded with emotion every time I hear the Lord's Prayer in Spanish. It reminds me of my childhood in Southern Arizona/Northern Mexico. I was raised on the Arizona side of Ambos Nogales, two border towns that share the same name, one Nogales in Arizona, the other in Sonora, Mexico. I regularly attended a Spanish Roman Catholic Mass with my mother in Nogales, Mexico. We would hold hands and say the Lord's Prayer in Spanish. Hearing the words *Padre*

Nuestro takes me home to the *elotero* selling corn and fruit just outside the church, the honking of the cars driving on the busy streets, and the people crossing themselves as they walk past the church.

I grew up along the border where language remains fluid. My sisters and I crossed into Nogales, Mexico with our mother most Saturdays to run errands. One of our stops was always the Roman Catholic Church. We would make the sign of the cross, visit the saint room, and admire the large, very detailed Nativity in December. As we grew taller we were able to reach the feet of more and more saints in the small dark room, and my mother always gave us change to put in the alms box as she knelt to pray.

On Sundays, while I was in elementary school, my sisters and I also attended Mass in Nogales, Sonora with my mother. I learned all the prayers in Spanish. I remember the large crowds of people and how by the middle of the Mass it was always standing room only. I also remember the kindness of the gentleman who sold fruit just outside on the day I felt faint during the service. He did not have water to offer me but he did have a large overturned bucket that I was invited to sit on.

During junior high, we made a change. Our entire family started to attend an English-speaking Mass in Nogales, Arizona, because my father refused to attend the Spanish Mass in Mexico. It started at noon. I remember sitting in the car parked outside the church waiting to hear which song was that week's number one on "American Top 40." As soon as the number one song was announced, we had to turn off the radio and rush into church. My mother did not speak English so she did not understand the sermon, but we felt like we were part of the Nogales, Arizona community during the service. We saw friends from school and I joined the choir with my neighborhood friends. This would end after my eighth grade year.

My family experienced a financial crisis after the Mexican peso devaluation of 1984. In the late summer of 1986, we moved to Tucson, Arizona, about sixty-five miles north of Nogales. It was a different world. I started high school in South Tucson and we no longer answered our home phone in Spanish. We rarely attended worship services even though my parents became involved in a prayer group that met one evening a week. Our weekly Saturday ritual of stopping at the church with our mother came to an end.

By the time I left for college on the East Coast, I had become un-churched. I was away from my family, away from my home, away from my faith. During my junior year of college my boy-friend and I decided that we were going to marry after I graduated. In preparation for marriage, I went through confirmation classes with the Roman Catholic chaplain at Wellesley College and was confirmed at the end of the school year. We spoke with a priest that summer to find out about getting married in the Roman Catholic Church, but in the end we did not feel that it was the home we were looking for. The Dean of Religious Life at Wellesley College, a priest in The Episcopal Church, officiated at our wedding on the day after my graduation.

After living in Northern California and attending an Episco-pal church there when our daughter was an infant, we moved back to Arizona, and decided to attend an Episcopal service in Span-ish in Phoenix. We were raising our three-year-old daughter as a monolingual Spanish-speaking toddler. While we started attend-ing church in Spanish again for our daughter, I actually recovered a missing piece of my spirituality. The Lord's Prayer in Spanish spoke to my heart. The music in Spanish filled my soul. I was home in The Episcopal Church, in a Spanish service, with my family.

Throughout the years our family has attended Spanish services as well as English ones. At times we have attended two services on a Sunday, one in English in the morning and one in Spanish around noon. The English service kept us informed about the happenings of the parish and the wider Episcopal Church and the Spanish service fed my soul. My childhood memories of my time in Nogales, Sonora—the songs, the prayers—all came flood-ing back. The mariachi music that many Spanish services in The Episcopal Church offer on a weekly basis always reminded me of the high holy days in the Roman Catholic Church, along with the festive holidays in the secular world in Mexico. My daughter and son know all the prayers in both Spanish and English.

In January 2007, my mother-in-law accompanied our family to the Basilica of the Virgin of Guadalupe in Mexico City. To witness her expression of wonder, belief, and love gazing at the Virgin's image is a memory that brings me great joy. The Virgin of Guadalupe, Mexico's patron saint, remains culturally and religiously significant for Latino/Mexican Episcopalians, and celebrating the Virgin's holy day, December 12th, continues to be a highlight of Advent festivities.

We also keep the celebration of posadas in The Episcopal Church. Posadas commemorate the journey of Mary and Jesus to Bethlehem. They are held the nine nights before Christmas, beginning on December 16th. They are celebrated in private homes, neighborhoods, and churches. The Episcopal Diocese of Arizona celebrated eight of the nine posadas at Latino Ministry congregations and each night we enjoyed a family reunion in a different part of the Phoenix metro area. After the celebration of the Eucharist, the children enjoyed breaking a piñata, while the adults feasted on traditional Mexican Christmas dishes (*posole, champurrado, flan, ponche*).

As a child, living on the border, in Ambos Nogales, I felt at home in both English and Spanish. Reconciling my Roman Catholic upbringing and Mexican culture to my family's life in The Episcopal Church has not always been seamless. We currently attend an English worship service at our local parish and remain involved in Latino Ministry on the church-wide level. We say the Lord's Prayer in our preferred language wherever we attend services.

Being bilingual remains an incredible gift that I received while being raised on the United States-Mexico border. I recently returned from a short trip to Panamá, where I attended a beautiful and inspiring bilingual worship service. Panamanians say the Lord's Prayer in both English and Spanish without any difficulty. It was so beautiful to hear the mixture of the languages. The singing in both languages gave me chills. We sang in English from The 1982 Hymnal, as well as traditional Spanish hymns. The service bulletin was printed in both English and Spanish and the sermon preached was bilingual. This experience of a truly bilingual worship service fed my Latina-Episcopalian soul.

On any given Sunday, the celebrant says, "Now in the words our Savior taught us, we are bold to say . . . ." I hold the hand of the person next to me in the pew and say *Padre Nuestro Que estas en el cielo* . . . . I think of holding my mother's hand as I learned that prayer. I think of holding my children's hands as they learned that prayer. I think of the gracious God whom I love and the Lord who gave us this prayer. I look around my church. I see my family. I am home.

18

Marriage and Worship

JOSEPH S. PAGANO

Worship saved my marriage.
 I'm not saying worship saved Amy and me from the normal run of marital problems like lack of communication, lack of intimacy, or financial stress. I suppose, in regard to these challenges, we have been relatively blessed in our twenty-eight years of married life. Then again, who knows, maybe regular participation in worship has helped there too. Just getting me up and shaved on Sunday mornings rather than sitting around in my boxer shorts until kickoff must have its benefits. But such help is more akin to studies that show regular church attendance adds two years to your life. That's not what I'm talking about when I say worship saved my

marriage. Worship has saved my marriage because it has placed Amy's and my intentions for love and faithfulness into the larger context of the triune God's love and faithfulness. Regular worship, whether I like it or not, interposes the small story of our married lives into God's great story of creation, redemption, and new life.

When Amy and I were married we made vows to one another in the presence of God and a gathered congregation. Amy's dad, a Lutheran pastor, presided, and in the opening address from the Book of Common Prayer reminded everybody what we were about in this worship service: "The bond and covenant of marriage was established by God in creation, and our Lord Jesus Christ adorned this manner of life by his presence and first miracle at a wedding in Cana of Galilee. It signifies to us the mystery of the union between Christ and his Church." Amy and I spoke words to each other meant to encompass all aspects of life: "for better for worse, for richer for poorer, in sickness and in health, to love and to cherish, until we are parted by death." Then we exchanged rings, and dared to speak to each other in the Name of God without being irreverent, blasphemous, or just plain foolish: "In the Name of God, I, Joseph, take you, Amy . . . . In the Name of God, I, Amy, take you, Joseph." Speaking our names, *Joseph, Amy,* in the Name of God made us acknowledge that we are bound together by God. We have no love, know no love, name no love outside of God's love. In the context of worship of the triune God, whom Martin Luther describes as "nothing but burning love and a glowing oven full of love,"[1] this is no bland sentimentality. The love of this God is dangerous, transformative, enticing. To worship such a God is to risk being consumed, purified, set ablaze. In the name of this God, we bound ourselves to each another in fear and trembling as well as in hope. So in accordance with the Book of Common Prayer, after we made our promises, and gave and received rings as signs of those promises, we did what anyone having made such huge and foolhardy promises ought to do: we knelt to pray.

The prayers in the marriage service focus not only on the newly married couple. They start with prayers for "the world you

1. Luther, *Werke* 36:425.

have made, and for which your Son gave his life," and they include prayers that "the bonds of our common humanity by which your children are united one to another and the living to the dead, may be so transformed by your grace, that your will may be done on earth as it is in heaven." Once again, we find the story of our lives plunked down into God's great story of creation, redemption, and new life. In between prayers for the world and prayers for everyone who has ever inhabited it, comes this petition: "Make their life together a sign of Christ's love to this sinful and broken world, that unity may overcome estrangement, forgiveness heal guilt, and joy conquer despair." In other words, the marriage liturgy is not just saying may these two people be held together in love. Rather, it says may they actually become—serve as—living icons of hope. May this couple standing before us and before God—where we can see them, even if we cannot gaze upon God directly—show us that Christ's love is so real, so powerful, so effective that estrangement, guilt, and despair don't stand a chance against unity, forgiveness, and joy. "See!" we say, looking at the couple in their wedding garments standing before the altar, "A sign that God is powerful, relentless, triumphant love."

Amy and I are both priests. We regularly serve together at Ash Wednesday services. Ash Wednesday marks the beginning of Lent, a season of penitence and fasting. Our Prayer Book tells us Lent "was also a time when those who, because of notorious sins, had been separated from the body of the faithful were reconciled by penitence and forgiveness, and restored to the fellowship of the Church. Thereby, the whole congregation was put in mind of the message of pardon and absolution set forth by the Gospel of our Savior, and of the need which all Christians continually have to renew their repentance and faith." I'd rather not think of myself and my marriage as in need of a "continual renewal of repentance and faith." I think I'm a pretty good husband: I do the grocery shopping, I help out with the chores around the house, I watch those awful British period dramas on PBS that Amy likes. What more can one expect?

After the congregation receives the imposition of ashes, Amy and I turn to each another. I stick my thumb into the container of ashes and grind it a bit so that the ashes cling to my skin. Then I take my thumb and trace a black sign of the cross on my wife's forehead and I say to her, "Remember that you are dust, and to dust you shall return." I do not like this. I don't like looking my wife in the eye and telling her that she is going to die. Every year I think this time I'll do it without my voice cracking and my eyes welling up with tears. And every year, my throat catches and the tears swell. The trouble is that these words are true. The liturgy forces me to be truthful with myself and with my wife about something I'd rather not acknowledge. It is such a stark truth. I wish we could ease our way into the whole truth-telling business. Couldn't we start with the ways I am a terrible passenger when Amy is driving? Not on Ash Wednesday. It's as if the liturgy is saying, "Let's get clear about this big truth up front. You are both going to die. Now we can get honest about the rest of your lives."

That is precisely what the Ash Wednesday service does. We say Psalm 51 (*Miserere mei, Deus*/Have mercy on me, O God) and then kneel for the Litany of Penitence. No one gets through this unscathed. We publicly confess to God and "to one another, and to the whole communion of saints in heaven and on earth, that we have sinned by our own fault in thought, word, and deed; by what we have done, and by what we have left undone." There is nowhere to hide as we confess our lack of love and forgiveness, the "pride, hypocrisy and impatience of our lives," our "dishonesty in daily life and work," and about a half dozen other types of sin.

Praying this litany within earshot of my wife is particularly bracing. We confess our "intemperate love of worldly goods and comforts." Left to my own devices, I might be able to convince myself that I lead a rather simple life. With my spouse kneeling beside me, I must confess the part of me that believes a new sixty-five-inch plasma television will bring marital bliss. Think of us, cuddling on the couch watching Masterpiece Theatre with those big English manor houses on such a big screen. We confess "our negligence in prayer and worship." I'm a priest. I'm in church all the time! Except my wife knows that for a long stretch during the 2016 presidential campaign I spent more time checking the morning news than saying Morning Prayer. We confess "our waste and pollution of God's creation, and our lack of concern for those who come after us." Ugghhh! Next to my wife I can't even get away with my slipshod recycling habits! The litany of penitence forces me to speak truthfully about my marriage whether I like it or not.

The only reason I can speak these truths is mindfulness of the promise also spoken of in the Ash Wednesday service: "the message of pardon and absolution set forth in the Gospel of our Savior." The litany ends with prayers that God's pardon and salvation be fulfilled in us. We pray: "Restore us, good Lord, and let your anger depart from us; favorably hear us, for your mercy is great. Accomplish in us the work of your salvation, that we may show forth your glory in the world. By the cross and passion of your Son our Lord, bring us with all your saints to the joy of his resurrection." The Ash Wednesday liturgy is framed by death and resurrection. I speak truthfully about my life and my marriage only as the Paschal Mystery is "accomplished in us." I don't know if I will ever be able to make the sign of the cross in ashes on my wife's forehead without choking up. Someday, however, I hope the tears of sorrow that come with the acknowledgment of our mortality will be mixed with tears of joy in the promise of resurrection.

Amy and I recently had the rare treat of worshipping together at All Saints' Chapel in Sewanee, Tennessee. We were at the School of Theology for a couple of weeks of continuing education as fellows in residence. It was All Saints' Day, a perfect time to be in a chapel named for this principal feast in the church year. I cherish the opportunity to sit in a pew next to Amy. Sometimes, it is sheer bliss to participate in worship without leading it. The liturgy was beautiful, the sermon very good, and the choir excellent. It had all I hope for on All Saints' when we pray in the collect of the day to the God who "has knit together your elect in one communion and fellowship in the mystical body of your Son Christ our Lord," and ask that "we may come to those ineffable joys that you have prepared for those who truly love you."

The closing hymn was "A Mighty Fortress." I croak along more or less in tune, but Amy sings like an angel. She sings this hymn by heart. Not only was her father a Lutheran pastor, but also her grandfather and her great-grandfather. I think of how many times she must have heard this hymn even before she was able to speak. Cradled in her mom's arms in the congregations her dad and her grandfather served, Luther's song of God's triumphant love must have pulsed in her tiny ears quickening a trust in God's promises that Luther knew God's word created even in infants. Then, as she grew, her own clear and true voice joined the congregation.

Amy's grandparents and parents are gone now, her mom and dad dying from cancer at ages far too young. I think of the gifted and gracious priest she has become and of how proud her parents would be of her. We sing "Let goods and kindred go, this mortal life also; the body they may kill, God's truth abideth still." Then it strikes me. It's not right to say that her parents *would be* proud of her, but rather that her parents *are* proud of her. It's All Saints' Day and we join our voices with angels and archangels and the whole company of heaven. Past, present, and future compress. Forebears, who sang *"Ein feste Burg,"* are now forerunners singing "A Mighty Fortress." A swirl of voices mingles with ours as the communion of saints draws us into their eternal praise and the souls of loved ones jostle alongside a dear one who sings a hymn she has heard since birth. My throat catches and tears flood my eyes. I can no longer sing, but am content to be in such goodly company. I want to be there always, in the presence of God, in the communion of saints, beside my wife, hearing her strong, clear song.

Worship saved my marriage.

Bibliography

Luther, Martin. *Martin Luthers Werke: Kritische Gesammtausgabe.* Weimar, Germany: Böhlau, 1883–2009.

19

Ashes

KATHRYN GREENE-MCCREIGHT

Creation

Almighty and everlasting God, you hate nothing you
have made and forgive the sins of all who are penitent:
Create and make in us new and contrite hearts, that we,
worthily lamenting our sins and acknowledging our
wretchedness may obtain of you, the God of all mercy,

perfect remission and forgiveness; through Jesus Christ
our Lord, who lives and reigns with you and the Holy
Spirit, one God, for ever and ever. Amen.

Thus opens the liturgy for Ash Wednesday: All things are good. All
is beloved by God. God hates nothing God created. God's nature is
to love, to be merciful, to forgive those who repent. God will create
in us new hearts, contrite wills through Jesus Christ. Nevertheless,
the words we most associate with Ash Wednesday are: *Remember
you are dust, and to dust you shall return.*

The most spiritually and emotionally difficult act for me as
a priest was the first time I imposed ashes on my children's foreheads. Our children are three-and-a-half years apart. Both entered
the world healthy, by the grace of God (when is it ever otherwise?).
But both were high-risk pregnancies. Contractions began at twenty-five weeks with our first and at eighteen weeks with our second.

Normal human gestation, so they say, lasts a biblical forty
weeks. Doctors use the term "viability" to indicate the gestational
age at which humans can ideally survive outside the womb. This
is usually thought to be somewhere around twenty-three weeks,
but babies delivered this early may be at risk of lifelong health
complications.

With both of our babies, I am reduced to a human incubator.
Everything I do centers around maintaining the pregnancies. Can
I walk up the hill to the Divinity School? No. Can I drive? No. Can
I shop? No. Cook? Stand? Sit? Take a shower? No. No. No. Once
a week.

I am not even allowed to attend childbirth classes. If I go in a
wheelchair? No! I have to spend my days in bed, lying as much as
possible on my left side. Sideways I study "What To Expect When
You're Expecting." (Certainly not this!) Sideways I memorize its
chart of average gestational fetal size and weight with each passing
week. Day by agonizingly long day.

Through my husband's feeding, coaxing, and attending to my
every need, along with my own fear, grit, and resolve, we manage
to keep each of our babies safely through gestation and birth, and
for the most part through healthy infancy. Our beautiful babies:

Noah, and later, Grace. How could they be otherwise named? But now this. Good God, you would have me smear a cross of ashes on those dear little foreheads?

Remember you are dust, and to dust you shall return.

The dust of Ash Wednesday. The ashes from the palms of last year's Triumphal Entry. Hosannas to the King at his joyful entry into Jerusalem. Yet even there, "In lowly pomp, ride on to die . . . ." Burned and sieved, the ashes are imposed with a mash of the thumb in the form of a cross onto the forehead. Make the ashes yourself sometime. Like making your own bread, it affords a deeper experience of the liturgy of the day.

We impose ashes, and yet it is dust that we are to remember on this day. Dust is the stuff of which we are made. In Genesis 2:7 we read that the LORD God forms our first parent (*'ādām*) through dust (*'āphār*) of the ground (*'adāmah*) itself and breathes into our nostrils the breath of life. This is how we, in our first parent, become living beings. Through dust and God's breath of life. Even and especially in our dustiness, we are created in the image of God.

Fall

The words at the imposition of ashes come from the curse the LORD God levies over the man in the Garden of Eden: "You are dust, and to dust you shall return" (Gen 3:19). But the man is only the third and final of the three main characters to hear their curse. First, the serpent; second, the woman; third, the man. The nature, content, and the simple fact that each character has their own specific curse are significant in setting up the narrative of the Scripture to follow.

Dust (*'āphār*) features in the first and final curses: on the serpent and on the man. The serpent is condemned to slither on its belly for the rest of its days and dust will be its food (Gen 3:14). But dust is not the man's food. It is his very beginning, middle, and end. And because we participate in our first parent's beginning, middle, and end, so we also share the curse. Dust is the realm of our existence, and of our end.

Remember you are dust, and to dust you shall return (Gen 3:19).

But while the curses on the serpent and on the man reduce them each in their own way to dust, the curse on the woman is different. Her curse is bracketed in the narrative by the dusty curses of these other two characters. On both sides of her curse, the dust chokes her fertility. The power she once had, along with the man, to fulfill God's earlier command to "be fruitful and multiply" (Gen 1:28) is now twisted. What was once blessing has now become bane. The woman will desire the man, yet her desire will bring pain in childbearing (Gen 3:16).

The same word for the dust (*'āphār*) of the first and last curses points the reader further ahead in the storyline: to the grave. And so Job cries: "Why do you not pardon my transgression and take away my iniquity? For now I shall lie in the earth (*'āphār*); you will seek me, but I shall not be" (Job 7:21). Dust is Israel's grave in their own punishment of exile. "There shall be a time of anguish, such as has never occurred since nations first came into existence. . . . Many of those who sleep in the dust of the earth (*'admat-'āphār*) shall awake, some to everlasting life, and some to shame and everlasting contempt" (Dan 12:2).

Dust is the stuff of mourning. The prototypical biblical act of mourning, throwing dust on one's head, recalls the breached and plundered Jerusalem. Dust is the grave of the Holy City. Even in its rubble, its very dust (*'āphār*), it is the beloved wreckage of the precious city of David (Ps 102:14). Deuteronomy 9 recounts the episode following the giving of the two tablets of the Law. There Moses is given the power to destroy the means by which the people have opposed God. He grinds the golden calf to dust, throwing its ashes into the stream. Moses stands in the breach on behalf of unfaithful Israel, protecting them from the LORD's righteous demands (Deut 9:21). Even while dust (*'āphār*) is a sign of judgment, it becomes, through Moses's righteous ministry, a sign of protection against the LORD's anger. Moses is a type of Christ here.

Promise

The Christian tradition sees in the curse the "first gospel," the pro-toevangelion (Gen 3:15). This first gospel precedes by several lines in the narrative the words that shape our Ash Wednesday liturgy. Dust here is a specifically theological signifier: death has met its match. The serpent, personifying death, will eat dust and dwell in the dust. He will be crushed under the foot of the Messiah: "He will strike your head, and you will strike his heel" (Gen 3:15). The saving grace of Jesus is foretold even in the curse on the serpent, the cause of our curses, even before the pronouncement of the curses on the woman and the man.

One of the most spiritually powerful illustrations of this first gospel that I have encountered was along the Camino de Santiago, the Way of St James. In the Middle Ages, the Camino was among the most important pilgrimage routes, third only to the routes to Jerusalem and to Rome. In the late twentieth and early twenty-first centuries, pilgrims have returned to its paths. In one of the churches along the Way, at the entrance to the nave stands a stone object about waist-high, eight-sided, with a shallow basin. Is it a font? Is it a stoop? Carved in relief at the bottom of the bowl's sloped sides is a stone snake, coiled as though ready to strike, half-submerged in holy water.

Dipping my fingers into the basin to cross myself, I inadvertently touch the stone snake. I feel it viscerally: the waters of baptism in which we die and rise with Christ have drowned our ancient foe. Yet they did not utterly destroy him. The serpent coiled at the bottom did indeed touch my fingers. But the Seed will crush its head. This is the promise: in the resurrection, "one little Word shall fell him." The now. The not yet. The yet to come. And so the dust of Ash Wednesday is seed, the promissory notes of our new life in Christ.

Remember you are dust, and to dust you shall return.

Fast-forward twelve years. We are visiting an ancient Italian city, unearthed in the mid-eighteenth century. It draws its fame from an "act of God" in 79 AD when the city's inhabitants tragically choked to death on ashes and dust in the eruption of Mount Vesuvius. Our Noah, whose only trace of pre-term birth is intermittent asthma, is an avid student of Latin poetry and ancient Roman history. "You and Dad are going so slow. Can't I just go and explore on my own?" We decide to let him wander at his own pace, agreeing that we would meet at the gift shop in one hour.

The time has come, we go to the gift shop, and look for Noah. We scour the shop. No Noah. Getting somewhat frustrated, we decide to divide and conquer. I stay in the shop while my husband goes to search the Forum. No Noah. We describe Noah to the clerk in the gift shop, but they have not seen him either. No Noah.

At this point I realize that we let him go off into the blistering summer heat of Pompeii without any water. I try to swallow my panic as I realize that Noah also does not have his asthma inhaler in his daypack. And he has no identification with him. This was before cell phones, so we cannot even phone him. I let my dear son, prone to asthma attacks in the dust of summer, go off without his inhaler? Without water? What kind of a mother am I? I now understand Mary's panic when she and Joseph can't find their son in another ancient city. At that point we frantically ask for the museum police.

Happy ending: there are two gift shops in Pompeii. Noah is in the one at the opposite end of the open-air museum. No heat stroke, no kidnapping, no asthma attack. Just one dusty, hot, grumpy Noah. "Where have you been?" he scolds. "I have been waiting for you for over an hour!"

Remember you are dust, and to dust you shall return.

20

Blessed Heroes

C. K. ROBERTSON

I stood at the altar, looking at faces familiar and new. I prefaced the final blessing as I have countless times before: "We are blessed so that we in turn might be a blessing to others." I then lifted my hand and said the familiar words, with the one addition I always used: "The blessing of Almighty God, Father, Son, and Holy Spirit, remain with you, *and shine out through you*, this day and always." The occasion was the funeral of my former parish administrator and dear friend. I had traveled back to St. Stephen's Church, Milledgeville, in the Diocese of Atlanta, where I had served as rector for several years. My successor had graciously invited me to share the service, giving me the privilege of offering the blessing at the end.

As I said those words, I found myself filled with emotion. I thought of my dear friend, yes, and of all those sitting before me. Like so many others on Sunday mornings in church pews throughout the country and across the globe, they had struggled at various times, in various ways, only to keep on waking up each day and daring to face the world. "Tribulation" is a word not often used in conversation, but I knew the very real tribulations that many of these dear souls had experienced. And yet, through triumphs and trials, through good times and bad, throughout it all, they kept showing up on Sunday mornings to be strengthened, renewed, refreshed: to be blessed. Then they would go forth and bless a whole lot of others around them. A few did so in visible, noteworthy ways, but most just shared words of encouragement and acts of kindness day after day after day. All of them made a difference, blessing others. To me, they were heroes all.

I grew up on heroes and the heroic. Every Sunday morning, before church, my dad and I would go to the local five & dime. Dad would get the Sunday newspaper and I would pick out a comic book to read after service. Through comic books, I first learned to read and, along the way, encountered intriguing characters who stood up for the helpless and inspired the hopeless.

These four-color protagonists first came to life at the onset of World War II, when economic catastrophe and real-life villains were, quite literally, threatening the world. The granddaddy of comic book heroes, Superman, was the brainchild of two young Jewish boys from Cleveland. He bore the same name as Nietzsche's *übermensch*, so much a part of Hitler's Aryan mythology. But there was no question that this Superman stood for truth and justice, fighting corrupt political bosses and perpetrators of domestic violence. More than this, Superman was a resident alien, a refugee, sole survivor of the doomed planet Krypton, sent off, like Moses, by his birth parents with the hope that he would find a new life in a land of possibilities, and make a difference in the lives of others. And then there was The Batman, a rich boy orphaned when his parents were gunned down in front of him, who made an oath to combat evil so no one else had to go through what he did. Fictional heroes like Superman and Batman inspired me as a youngster because they were committed to showing up and making a difference.

It's not just fictional characters who pointed me toward the heroic. I am a lifelong baseball fan and a proud, card-carrying member of the Hall of Fame in Cooperstown. However, I let others cheer loudly for the home run kings, the ones who seem to possess almost supernatural power as they swing the bat and watch the ball soar into the distance. For me, Lou Gehrig of the New York Yankees and Cal Ripken, Jr. of the Baltimore Orioles, the "Iron Men" of baseball, were the real heroes. Both boasted impressive records, but for each the greatest accomplishment was showing up on the field every game, doing what was needed, despite whatever injuries or illness they faced, day in and day out.

I still remember the night when Ripken surpassed Gehrig's long-standing record for most consecutive games played. It came at a dire time for baseball, when a players' strike had shut down the previous season. Many people had given up on the sport, disgusted and disillusioned with how business self-interest had co-opted the National Pastime.

On that glorious night the following summer, midway through the game, the record was officially reached. Play on the field stopped, dignitaries made speeches, and officials presented awards, all carefully choreographed beforehand. Then something spontaneous occurred. The crowd rose for a standing ovation and didn't sit down. They stood, clapping for over twenty minutes, and a surprised but appreciative Ripken was called to do a victory lap. He ran around the edges of the ballpark, shaking hands with fans while the cheering persisted. It is said that the home run king Babe Ruth saved baseball after the infamous Black Sox scandal of 1919. In September of 1995, Cal Ripken, Jr. saved baseball again, not by hitting home runs (though he did knock out a solo four-bagger on that special night), but instead by showing up and making a difference again and again, in 2,131 consecutive games.

There is another reminder of the heroic in the back of my mind every time I say the words of the Blessing. When I was growing up my family had its routines and rhythms. Most Sundays, after church we headed over to the donut shop and picked out a dozen to take home. But once a month, every month, my dad, a World War II veteran, would drive us from our Maryland parish across the Potomac River to the Ft. Myers army base. I would, of course, read my comic book-of-the-week along the way. There we would enjoy a brunch at the officer's club. It was a sumptuous feast each time, with a large ice sculpture in the middle of the room, surrounded by eggs and grits, pancakes and waffles, sausage and bacon, fruits and pastries of every kind, and, to top it all off, a separate dessert table. Afterwards, we would take a long walk onto the adjoining grounds of Arlington National Cemetery, timing our walk so we would arrive a few minutes before the hourly Changing of the Guard at the Tomb of the Unknown Soldier. No matter how many times I experienced this, I found myself entranced by the ceremony: the precision marching, the click-click-click of the honor guards' heels, the salutes offered before the tomb, the solemnity of the moment. What impressed me most of all was the fact that all this ceremony was done not to honor a president or recognized leader, but rather to honor unnamed soldiers "known only to God," ordinary people who showed up every day to do their duty.

For me, the heroic really is not about abilities, power, or status, but showing up and making a difference. The Baptismal Covenant includes the words "with God's help" after each pledge is made: "Will you continue in the apostles' teaching . . . persevere in resisting evil . . . proclaim by word and example . . . seek and serve Christ in all persons . . . strive for justice and peace?" "I will, *with God's help*." We are called to a life of service in Christ's Name, but always with God's help. We are called to be a blessing to others, but always because we are assured that God is already at work blessing us, strengthening us, helping us through the Spirit to put one foot in front of the other and, as the apostle Paul put it, to "press on." I love the Eucharist, the sermon, the prayers, and hymns. But for me the great privilege every Sunday morning is to offer the Blessing and hear the accompanying Dismissal, as the people of God—heroes all—are sent forth to show up and make a difference in the lives of all around us, day after day after day.

21

A Beautiful Inheritance

AMY PETERSON

We spent all day cleaning. I scrubbed the mineral build-up from the faucet with a toothbrush while Jack swept the faux-wood floors and our two tiny children conquered the pile of shoes and jackets by the door. After a quick dinner—pizza on paper plates, to keep the cleaned kitchen clean—the first tentative knock at the door signaled the beginning of our celebration.

We'd invited friends and colleagues, anyone who over the past three years had helped us make a place in rural Indiana, to join us in the liturgy of "Celebration for a Home" from the Book of

Occasional Services. Cars parked along our long gravel driveway. Leaving their shoes at the door, people padded in ones and twos into the kitchen, where cider and cocoa simmered on the stove. Renata warmed her fingers around a heavy mug and exclaimed at the view. "If my kitchen window looked out on that, I might never stop doing dishes," she said.

She's right: it's a good view. Our neighbors to the left bale hay, and our neighbors to the right alternate soybeans and corn. We are in flat farm country, but at the back of our two acres, the land slopes gently upward into a wooded hill, one of the only undulations for miles. The sun rises over that hill. We sometimes see deer emerge from its woods to gnaw on the trunks of our white pines, and we sometimes hear the howl of wolves. It might be because of the view from the back porch that we bought this house.

I'd never wanted to buy a house. By the time my husband and I got around to thinking about mortgages and realtors, we were well into our thirties, and I felt no small measure of trepidation about it all. It wasn't just the financial investment that scared me, though—I worried constantly about what it meant to spend money on the things of middle-class American identity in a world in which inequality reigned. I also worried that in buying this house, we were committing to stay in one place for a while. I worried that we might put down roots.

I'd never wanted to put down roots, either. Over the last decade, I had moved every couple of years. I had lived in two foreign countries. I had been able to fit all my belongings into the back of my car. I liked that sort of freedom; and there were still so many places that I wanted to see.

Of all the places I'd lived, northern Indiana seemed the least likely candidate for a long-term home. We had no family in the area, and Hoosier culture often felt to me as foreign as any of the Asian and European countries I'd sojourned through in my twenties. Yet after three years renting, we were buying a house instead of leaving. Part of the reason we felt able to do that was because of the home we'd found in our church, a small Episcopal congregation in the next town over. And so it seemed fitting, and even necessary: if we were going to commit to a house, we should commit with our spiritual community promising to help.

Father Jim passed photocopied liturgies around. Ethan, the only teenager present, stood next to him holding the holy water Jim would sprinkle on each room. People balanced their pages on cups of hot chocolate and conversation quieted. We circled up.

Grasping a heavy Bible, Jack turned to Genesis 18, and read about Abraham's hospitality to the three strangers who appeared to him in his tent under the oaks of Mamre. Abraham invited them to rest, wash, and eat, and asked Sarah to make fresh bread for the visitors. He selected a calf for a servant to prepare for them, and then he stood with them while they ate.

The appointed reading stops there, and feels oddly truncated. We know what comes next, but it remains unsaid, as if the liturgy wants us to remember that this is just the first part of the story for us, too. This is the part where you open your heart to the LORD as the LORD appears, suddenly, within your tents. The part with the blessing, the surprise, the laughter, the disbelief; the warning, the pleading, the bargaining, the blessing—all that is still to come. Tonight is for the welcoming and the feasting, and the reminder that our doors are to stay open.

Our socked feet slipped from room to room as the liturgy continued. We became a herd of worshippers and friends sidling next to each other in the office, the bedroom, the playroom, the kitchen, for prayers. Owen, my two-year-old son, and his best friend Charlie ran headlong from one side of the house to the other, and back again, pretending to be Batman and Robin. We kept praying. Before long Rosie, who was four, had changed into her Supergirl costume and joined them.

As we chanted the prayers, I wondered what the Christians from my childhood would think of this ritual. I grew up with low-church traditions: we popcorn-ed our prayers and we did not believe in symbols. We were gnostics, in many ways, and it wouldn't have occurred to us to pray a blessing over rag rugs and faux-wooden floors and smudged windows; if we'd heard that people in some other church prayed such prayers, we'd have thought them silly and superstitious.

The religious people I had met in Cambodia would have loved our house-blessing. In Cambodia, I had friends for whom the spiritual and the physical were so deeply intertwined that they could never be untangled. My Buddhist friends believed in correspondence between physical and spiritual realities. They lit candles for their ancestors, and left food for them, and sometimes at night they drove without headlights so as not to draw the attention of evil spirits. From them I had begun to understand what it meant to fear God, to be a participant in mystery, and to believe that the physical world and the spiritual world were not separate spheres.

How would I explain this ritual to the Christians from my childhood, though? I would tell them that this isn't superstition; we're not here because we think ghosts and evil spirits haunt our home and an incantation can ward them off. This isn't about good-luck charms, a horseshoe hanging over the door or a double happiness symbol bringing fortune. And yet it isn't quite true to say that there is no magic here; we do believe in spirits. We do believe in the power of words and of the Word.

These prayers are a way of reminding ourselves of the truth. Remembering

- in the office, that God is the source of wisdom;
- in the bedroom, that we can sleep in peace because God alone makes us dwell in safety;
- in the children's rooms, that Jesus called the little ones to himself;
- in the kitchen, that God supplies all of our needs;
- in the guest room, that by showing hospitality, some have entertained angels unawares.

We are reminded that the physical world matters, and that our home is not ours alone. "Open your homes to each other without complaining," the liturgy commands. "Use the gifts you have received from God for the good of others."

When the prayers finish, we slice cheesecake and gather in clusters around the table and the bookshelves. I put Denison Witmer on the record player and find a book of poetry that Karen has asked to borrow. Eventually the children go to bed, and Jack and some guys head to the back of the property to talk around the bonfire. The moon is full tonight. I wash dishes and consider the view out the window, then add whisky to my cider and take a book to bed with me.

This isn't the house I would have chosen, nor the town, nor the job. I would have gone with an older house, a more ethnically diverse city, a job where I got to feel like I was saving the world everyday.

But last week I told this house that I would be happy to grow older with it. Every day I thank the chickens for giving me their eggs, and I've mowed the grass often enough now that I'm learning where the ground is level and where it slants, where the milkweed pods grow and what the names of the trees are. I am learning to put my faith in the slow-growth of leaves rotting into compost and relationships ripening into richness. I am trying, in this time, to know my place, to know myself, and in that to flourish in the obscurity of middle America.

So this is our house, our home; this is our field—or we are its. We celebrate a home through liturgy not because we are superstitious but because we need help learning to be grateful, learning to live in the LORD's world and to share it with the community that surrounds us. The prayers are a reminder that here, for a minute, maybe, we can image the eternal home for which we hope.

The lines have fallen for me in pleasant places;
indeed, I have a beautiful inheritance. (Psalm 16:6)

22

God Bless Rocket and Bobo and Tigger

RACHEL MARIE STONE

I am a little embarrassed to admit how much I love the Blessing of the Animals. An educated adult, a mother, a teacher should count Tenebrae, or Ash Wednesday, or Easter Morning, or Christmas Eve, among her favorites: services with longer histories and greater significance, but, if I'm being honest, the service that I really look forward to, savor, and reflect upon with satisfaction is the one held in honor of St. Francis. I could tell you that this is because my firstborn child, Aidan, himself an animal lover, was born on October 4, Blessed Francis's feast day, but the truth is that I just really love bringing one of my pets to church.

As a child growing up in a tradition that was next door to Puritanism, I read about the hours-long services of Puritan New England and how, in winter, congregants might bring dogs along to warm their feet. *What fun*, I thought. Not only would you be warmer, but the dog would provide companionship and maybe a bit of a welcome distraction from those endless sermons. (Perhaps my drift toward the Canterbury trail, with its much shorter homilies, was inevitable.) I've never owned a pet stroller or a handbag designed to accommodate a dog, nor do I bring my pets along on shopping trips or social calls. But even as a preschooler I expressed my preference for the historic Tenth Presbyterian Church in Philadelphia because they had a guinea pig in the children's room. In elementary school I always wanted to sit near the class hamster. I remember almost nothing about third grade except that for a brief time we kept caterpillars, and then the butterflies they became, on the corner of our desks, and I floated through those days with unspeakable joy. I begged my parents to be allowed to train seeing eye dogs and dreamed, in case that didn't work, of having a disability just severe enough to require the omnipresence of a sweet Labrador.

Minimally, then, the Blessing of the Animals indulges my childish longing to bring a pet with me everywhere, even church. I feel relaxed and happier with my cat on my lap or my dog at my feet, and I suspect that's how lots of pet owners feel, and if that partly explains the swelled attendance at the Blessing of the Animals. I wonder how many more people would attend morning worship regularly if they could bring their dog with them every time. Our parish welcomes actual pets inside the building—not just photographs of pets, as in some parishes—and because the date tends to coincide with a neighborhood fair, our priest offers open-air blessings as well. People in the neighborhood have become regular parishioners after seeking a blessing for their dogs and cats and chinchillas.

I love watching the faces of the congregants on that day. As they carry small dogs and lead larger ones, as they lug crates with cats or rabbits or box turtles, I recognize a look of pride and amusement, of affection and something like satisfaction. It's as if everyone has brought a part of themselves to church that's usually left at home: the part that crochets on the couch whilst wearing pajamas and watching crime dramas; the part that reads middle-brow genre fiction in bed, hair askew; the part that fusses over animals in a high pitched voice that they'd never use at the office or at church. It's as if our souls have come to church in their slippers and bathrobes. We're less guarded, because how sophisticated and dignified can you be when you're cradling a floppy-eared puppy, or toting a bunny in a box? I love that the service opens up—and shares—something in us that's usually reserved for home.

For similar reasons, I appreciate the inevitable howling of some of the dogs during the congregational singing. Yes, canine friends: some of us are more tuneless than a blender, and we are not deterred in making our joyful noise unto the Lord. If the dogs are howling in pain, of course, I would not want to laugh at this, but from my observations, it seems that much of the howling is rather an attempt at joining in song, and when one dog starts, others join in. I love the variety of their howls—some deep, some high, some resonant, others thin—and it is so like (human) congregational singing that I can hardly keep it together: the way one starts and the rest chime in, with varying degrees of musicality. I like the frankness with which the dogs howl and their utter lack of decorum. This is also why I appreciate the presence of babies and small children in congregational worship, with their honest bluntness ("*I'm hungry*," "I wanna *go!*" "He's *old!*" "*Amen!*"). I wonder what congregational worship would be like if we were all a little less self-conscious. I like how dogs and children are unafraid to sing themselves, as Walt Whitman might have said, and I like to see the owners' amused embarrassment at their dogs' "singing." I wish we all sang as bravely as our dogs do.

When the actual blessing part of the service begins, I crane my neck to see and hear, like little kids do when there's a baptism.

It delights me that the liturgy specifically calls for the celebrant to bless the pet *by name*: "N. (name of animal, i.e., 'Smokey,' not cat/dog)."

It reminds me of my childhood misunderstanding of Adam naming the animals. I imagined that he sat there on a big rock saying, "Hey, I'm gonna call you Rascal! And you're gonna be Rosie. And this one is Wilbur!" No, no, my dad said, gently, the story meant to convey the idea that Adam named them "raccoon," "cow," and "pig." How impersonal and boring, I thought. I love the combination of the dignified and the absurd in the prescribed liturgy of a formal blessing *by name* for each little Rocket and Bobo and Tigger. I love how it brings together our desire for spiritual understanding and divine blessing and orderly worship with the simple pleasure we take in our howling, meowing, and generally undignified creatures. I love the particularity: the priest is not blessing *all* creatures, but rather Micky, Misty, Socks, Tweety, Molly, Percy. We might talk of loving "creation," which is really too general to picture. I always picture a photograph of earth from space, which is too abstract to love. But a dog isn't, and it seems to be the way of humans that we can only really hate in abstraction, and love in particulars.

One could criticize as hypocrisy the fact that people bring pampered pets to be blessed even as their own bellies are digesting meat, milk, and eggs from factory-farmed animals who suffer terrible cruelties, or one could point out how much better fed the average American domestic animal is than many people in the world. There may be justice in these accusations. Still, it is hard to loathe or love "animals" or even "dogs"; we might find ourselves disarmed by encountering sweet Percy or playful Molly. Acknowledging the goodness and individuality of highly particular animals seems to be a good way to begin caring for animals more generally. Love is particular, and is inclined to overspill its bounds.

I find it especially moving to see old pets at the Blessing of the Animals: the bony, arthritic cats, limping, graying dogs, sometimes accompanied by owners whose frailties seem to match. *What does the blessing mean?* I find myself wondering, not just this blessing but every blessing. When I was very young, I prayed fervently for a miraculous cure for my kitten, who was dying of feline immunodeficiency virus. I no longer think that such intercessions are the primary work of prayer, but I'm not always sure what prayer—and blessings—really are *for*. Are we trying to talk God into something? Are we expecting miraculous healing, or the reversal of time's inevitable decay? Fairy tales are full of warnings about wishing for such things. So what are we seeking when we bring our old, sick pets to be blessed?

I think of what the dying minister John Ames wrote to his son in Marilynne Robinson's *Gilead*, about an episode in his childhood when he and his friends, "very pious children from pious households in a fairly pious town," baptized a litter of cats:

> I still remember how those warm little brows felt under the palm of my hand. Everyone has petted a cat, but to touch one like that, with the pure intention of blessing it, is a very different thing. It stays the mind. For years we would wonder what, from a cosmic viewpoint, we had done to them. It still seems to me to be a real question. There is a reality in blessing. . . . It doesn't enhance sacredness, but it acknowledges it, and there is a power in that. I have felt it pass through me, so to speak. The sensation is one of really knowing a creature, I mean really feeling its mysterious life and your own mysterious life at the same time.[1]

Later, Ames's father—also a minister—admonishes his son that the sacraments must be treated with the greatest respect. Of course the child John Ames respected the sacraments—but, he writes, "we thought the whole world of those cats."[2]

I think most of us are like that: we still wonder what, from a cosmic viewpoint, the blessing really means. What has been done to us in baptism? What do we get when we receive the Eucharist? What happens when we are pardoned? When we cross ourselves, when we kneel? We are reminded, again and again, that we are

1. Robinson, *Gilead*, 23.
2. Robinson, *Gilead*, 23.

beloved creatures with serious obligations toward and connections with other beloved creatures. We relish existence at its most elemental: water, wine, bread, sin, reconciliation, peace. Like our animals, we are often unsure why we've been dragged—or have dragged ourselves—out of the comfort of home and into church. Maybe we're there just for a touch and a word that acknowledges holiness, even if, like the dogs and cats, we don't exactly know what it all really means.

Bibliography

Robinson, Marilynne. *Gilead.* New York: Picador, 2004.

23

The Priest in the Trees

FRED BAHNSON

On the last Sunday in September 2015, the Reverend Stephen Blackmer stopped beside the stand of beech stumps where he had once performed the chain-saw Eucharist. He was leading a dozen or so members of the Church of the Woods on a contemplative walk and had invited me along. With his plaid shirt, decades-old custom Limmer hiking boots, and graying beard sans mustache, Blackmer didn't look the part of an Episcopal priest. He skipped nimbly over roots and rocks, turning around to laugh or make a point. His talk swept from exuberant to pensive to crass;

at times he sounded like the theologically astute priest he was, at others like a mischievous wood sprite.

It was the first anniversary of the church, located several miles from the town of Canterbury, New Hampshire. A full lunar eclipse was expected that night, and Blackmer would be turning sixty in a few days. To celebrate these auspicious events, church members had planned a full day of activities: meditation walks, trail work, a Eucharist service, a bonfire, and, for those who still had energy, an eclipse-viewing party. When the group paused along the ridge of beech stumps it was midmorning; they were only halfway through a circumnavigation of the church's 106 acres, which Blackmer described as a "labyrinth on a grand scale." There was no church building, just woods. If you wanted to see the sanctuary, you had to hike.

The contemplative trek would take around three hours, but no one was complaining. Long walks in the woods are conducive to stories. Like the story of the chain-saw Eucharist. On a sunny, twelve-degree day in January, Blackmer had hiked into the Church of the Woods pulling a sled full of trail-clearing gear: axe, chain saw, oil, and gas. He wanted to clear new meditation trails, which mostly involved sawing up blowdowns and saplings. When he came to the ridge, he found it choked by the stand of young beech, so he cranked up his Jonsered and began felling trees. Over the next hour, Blackmer had a growing feeling that something wasn't right. He hit the kill switch. *Shit*, he thought, *I have utterly sinned and fallen short of the glory of God.* It wasn't cutting trees that bothered him. It was that he had been taking life after life "and had been utterly oblivious to the enormity of that act." He had failed to remember that trees, even scrubby little saplings, are worthy of reverence.

Blackmer's sled also held what he called his prayer kit: Communion bread, a water bottle full of wine, the Book of Common Prayer. Kneeling in the sawdust and snow beside one of the widest stumps, he spread out the elements and set up an altar. That day's lectionary reading was from Isaiah. He read aloud: "I have swept away your transgressions like a cloud, and your sins like mist.

Return to me, for I have redeemed you. . . . Shout, O depths of the earth! Break forth into singing, O mountains, O forest, and every tree in it." He prayed the prayer of confession, consecrated the bread and wine, and offered them to his fellow congregants—the trees—before partaking himself.

Before he became an Episcopal priest Blackmer spent thirty years as a forest ecologist and conservationist. For most of his life he'd been an agnostic. When he first read the Bible as an adult, he was struck by how often the biblical writers engaged the very subject he'd spent his career studying: the land. The places in which the narrative occurred—mountaintops, hillsides, lakeshores, gardens—were not just stages on which the human story played out; they were actors in the story itself. He came to love the Psalms, and the frequency with which the psalmist used metaphors of nature, especially trees. Blackmer quoted from Psalm 92: "The righteous ones flourish like the palm tree. . . . They are planted in the house of the LORD. . . . In old age they still produce fruit; they are always green and full of sap." He went on to describe how in other psalms the trees of the fields clap their hands and shout for joy. "When humans sing praises," he said, "we do the same thing." Nature is not inert. It was a revelatory idea.

In the Gospels, Blackmer found the most intriguing examples of divine encounter in nature. He kept noticing what he called "throwaway lines": after Jesus had "dismissed the crowds, he went up the mountain by himself to pray" (Matthew), or "He would withdraw to deserted places and pray" (Luke). Sometimes Jesus went to a garden. Or a lakeshore. Or the Judean desert. The location varied, but the pattern was evident throughout the Gospels. Jesus went to the temple "to teach and to raise a ruckus," but when he needed to pray Jesus fled to the countryside, to places unmediated by both temples and the religious authorities that governed them. These epiphanies gave Blackmer an idea: why not bring worship out into the woods? "Of course one can experience God in a building," he told me. But for at least some people, especially at this time of climate change, there needs to be a practice of going into the wilderness to pray. And if one lives in New England, the obvious place to do that is the woods.

Church of the Woods is affiliated with The Episcopal Church, as well as a non-profit organization called Kairos Earth, which Blackmer founded in 2013. In biblical Greek, *kairos* refers to an opportune or critical moment when God acts. In its first year, nearly nine hundred people attended services at the Church of the Woods. Of its thirty or so regular members, nearly half have graduate degrees. Many are medical professionals whose finely tuned diagnostic skills tell them that our planet is running a fever. As one woman, a Harvard-trained research physician, told me, "Climate change is the biggest public health crisis humanity has ever faced." Blackmer believes our ecological crises have precipitated a *kairos* moment. He sees a parallel with the Book of Jeremiah, in which the prophet describes a sense of impending doom as the Babylonians laid siege to Jerusalem in 587 BC. "I looked on the earth, and lo, it was waste and void," Jeremiah wrote, "and to the heavens, and they had no light." On reading the book in seminary, Blackmer's first thought had been, *He's talking about climate change.*

As Western Christianity undergoes its identity crisis—a reformation or a slow implosion, depending on your leaning—a small but determined number of people like Blackmer are urging the church to seek God in the literal wilderness. They are calling for carbon repentance, but their credo is more nuanced than just slapping a fresh coat of Christian morality onto secular environmental politics; the Sierra Club at prayer this is not. At the Church of the Woods there is no action plan, no hive of online activity promising the earth's salvation if only you *click here.* There is rather a summons, an invitation to carry the church's liturgy into one's local ecosystem and thereby rediscover the awe and wonder that Moses experienced before the burning bush. By wooing Christianity back to its feral beginnings, Blackmer believes, we can finally confront the long trajectory of our ecological sin, and perhaps begin to turn.

The forest trekkers arrived at the Altar, a small clearing where the church holds its services. The altar itself is a white-pine stump festooned with British soldier moss. Someone counted the rings and reported that the tree was more than ninety years old. One member placed Indian cucumber on the altar as an offering, another set down a reishi mushroom.

The Altar is the spiritual, if not the actual, center of the church. It is here that Blackmer offers Communion to his peripatetic flock. There is a worry among certain mainline Christians that once you start dabbling in nature, you're on the slippery slope to paganism, but Blackmer is no druid. He found years ago that the vague, earth-based spirituality he'd lived with for most of his life wasn't enough, and now considers himself a solid Trinitarian.

Many of the members at Church of the Woods are either former or current environmental activists. One woman helped form a non-profit that fought a protracted legal battle against a lumber company that wanted to develop 400,000 acres of Maine woods. Another was arrested alongside the environmentalist Bill McKibben at a rally against the Keystone XL pipeline in 2011. Blackmer fully supports lobbying and activism, but a common theme among members of Church of the Woods is that activism isn't enough. This need to find a new path through liturgy and contemplation was true both of seasoned activists like Blackmer and younger church members who had looked at the available activist responses to the ecological crisis—secular or faith-based—and found them wanting. When Blackmer considered the difference between Christians protesting a coal plant and secular activists doing the same, he thought, *There has to be something different in liturgy,* giving the word its full extent of meaning in New Testament Greek. *Leitourgia* gets translated as "worship or service to God," but it can also be understood as "the work of the people."

Following a long respite at the Altar, we arrived at a fork in the trail. Blackmer stooped, picked a handful of wintergreen leaves from the understory, and passed them around for us to chew. We nibbled, walked, and prayed.

The story of Moses and the burning bush is one of Blackmer's favorite texts. In Exodus, the Lord appears to Moses in a bush that burns but is not consumed. "Remove the sandals from your feet, for the place on which you are standing is holy ground." Blackmer often takes that literally, celebrating the Eucharist barefoot. Confronted with the threat of climate change, he believes, we must think of all ground as holy ground. Without such a recognition, there is no way out of our ecological woes. In the Eastern Orthodox tradition, the burning bush prefigures Mary the Theotokos, the God-bearer, who carried the Incarnate God inside her womb but remained unharmed. Blackmer thinks of the Earth itself as a *theotokos*. Would we clear-cut a forest or demolish a mountain or frack a field that bore the living God?

When our little band of pilgrims returned to the parking lot, Blackmer pointed out the church's sole "relic," a bent and broken aluminum ladder leaning against a tree, left behind by the loggers when they high-graded the place. It reminds him of Jacob's Ladder, another favorite biblical story. Genesis recounts how Jacob lay down upon a stone to sleep and dreamed of a ladder that joined heaven and earth. Upon awakening, he exclaimed, "Surely the LORD is in this place—and I did not know it!"

A common theme in Blackmer's conversations is that we've lost the face-to-face connection with God, the awesome, fearsome encounter that so often occurs in wild settings. Art, music, a beautiful sanctuary—all of those can be soul-stirring. But they can also obfuscate one's connection to God. Nature strips away the human intermediary.

Since the Industrial Revolution we've scaled up development to a tremendous degree, and even under the most optimistic scenarios we're going to be dealing with climate change for centuries to come. Blackmer foresees a time of unimaginable suffering and grief. His faith tells him that on the far side of that suffering stands the tree of life, symbol of the resurrected world in which humans will have found their place in creation. There is no path to that perfect world, however, that does not involve hardship and death. "We're not going to skate through this one untouched," he told me.

Though Blackmer freely acknowledges that some are called to activism and that such work is sorely needed, he himself has left that role behind, at least in the usual sense. Activism, in his view, too often becomes a mask for hiding undigested fear or grief. His work now is to change people's consciousness rather than to affect policy.

Hearing Blackmer talk, one might wonder how a shift in consciousness can save a beleaguered planet. As environmental groups like 350.org have shown, it takes direct political action to achieve tangible results, such as the protests that managed to stop the construction of the Keystone XL pipeline, or Blackmer's own efforts to preserve millions of acres of New England forest. It's difficult to imagine achieving those results through an internal shift, but for Blackmer, the emphasis is on the activist's starting place. The question is not whether one takes action, it is from what heart and mind one does so.

The church's *leitourgia*, the work of the people, is first the work of prayer. The once thriving Canterbury Shaker Village lies only a few miles east of the Church of the Woods, and for Blackmer the proximity is no coincidence. The Shakers's connection to the land and their devotion to prayer left a spiritual presence that is still palpable. "Prayer transforms places as well as people," Blackmer said. "You can actually feel it when you walk into a place where people have prayed for long periods of time. It is as if prayer has changed the molecular structure of a place." Thus altered, the woods become a kind of inner sanctum in which we are faced with what the theologian Rudolf Otto called the *mysterium tremendum.* "The semi-darkness . . . of a lofty forest glade," he wrote in *The Idea of the Holy*, "has always spoken eloquently to the soul, and builders of temples, mosques, and churches have made full use of it."[1]

The work of the people also includes the Eucharist. For Blackmer, "It is the act of taking into ourselves the body of He who died and went through death and came back." Death and grief transmuted into love. That expression of hope in the midst of death is where, for Blackmer, the Christian faith comes into its own. "All of

1. Otto, *The Idea of the Holy*, 68.

us go down to the dust," he said, quoting the burial rite from the Book of Common Prayer, "yet even at the grave we make our song: Alleluia, alleluia, alleluia." Death does not have the final word. Joy does. "That's what Jesus was all about," Blackmer said. "And if we forget that, then shit—we're a sad, pitiful bunch. And we're sure as hell not leading anybody to the Promised Land." When he presides over the liturgy each Sunday, this priest in the trees, a sixty-one-year-old man still green and full of sap, carefully spreads his elements across the white-pine stump. The first morsels of bread and the last sip of wine he offers to the earth.

Clearly the church's liturgy gives shape to our religious imaginations, but can it really help us confront climate change? Perhaps, but only if we allow our liturgical life to be shaped and challenged by the ecological imagination. If we do, we would be rooting ourselves more deeply in the biblical tradition, for the redemption of God's people cannot be separated from the redemption of the land. The search for God in a sacred grove recalls the Israelites in their tabernacle in the Sinai desert, a search that cannot be contained by human walls, despite the solidity that Chartres or Notre Dame or the National Cathedral might suggest. If Christianity is going to confront climate change, perhaps it needs to rewild itself, to go feral. What the faith has to offer first is not protest or activism, people like Blackmer show us, though it may lead there. It is *leitourgia*. The work of the people. And the work of the people now is this: Keep the land holy. Keep the carbon in the ground. Renounce the myth that this earth is a random assortment of bio-geophysical processes that can be prodded, manipulated, fracked, or drilled for our own purposes, however nefarious or benign. Let us approach with awe the *theotokos*, the bush that burns but is not consumed. Perhaps we begin by taking off our shoes.

Bibliography

Otto, Rudolf. *The Idea of the Holy*. 2nd ed. New York: Oxford University Press, 1958.

Made in the USA
Columbia, SC
09 June 2020